EDMOND JAL[OUX]

THE EVOLUTION OF

D0559434

Marthe Rose[nfeld]

This book traces the development of Edmond Jaloux (1878-1949) from his beginnings as a follower of naturalism, through a stage of poetic imagination, to a last period in which he sought to recreate supernatural and imaginary worlds.

It revises the conventional estimate of Edmond Jaloux that marked him as a writer of escapist literature. Jaloux has been represented as a seeker of phantasy, whose novels reflect the impact of the waning Symbolist movement. Symbolism, however, influenced only one stage of his development as a novelist. A comprehensive view of Edmond Jaloux's evolution shows that his period of poetic imagination was followed by a time of greater inwardness, which characterized the last years of his career. For the latter stage was increasingly marked by mysticism and the quest after a transcendent reality.

Jaloux's spiritual journey is significant not only because it determines his place in French literature. It illuminates also the principal literary and philosophical movements of the first half of the twentieth century. This search for absolute values in art epitomizes the yearning of the generation of 1900 for permanent truths in an age of impermanence, relativity and revolutionary upheaval.

A native of Belgium, Marthe Rosenfeld studied in the United States, and earned the Ph.D. degree at New York University. During 1960-1962 she was a Fulbright scholar at the Sorbonne. She has taught at Wilson College and Boston University, and is currently an Assistant Professor of French at Indiana University at Fort Wayne.

EDMOND JALOUX:
THE EVOLUTION OF A NOVELIST

EDMOND JALOUX:

THE EVOLUTION OF A NOVELIST

by

MARTHE ROSENFELD

With a Foreword by

GABRIEL MARCEL

PHILOSOPHICAL LIBRARY

NEW YORK

Printed in the United States of America

FOREWORD

The author of this work has put literary scholars in her debt by devoting to the fiction of Edmond Jaloux a study that is thoroughly researched and carefully thought out, and of the kind that we do not possess in France. This book serves, in my opinion, as a just compensation, for I feel that neither the originality of Jaloux's novels, nor their other qualities, have been fully recognized up to now. The critics have been content merely to apply labels to him, or to see him as a follower, when in fact the lifelong quest that he carried on from his earliest works to *Le Culte secret* and *Le Pays des fantômes* should have elicited an attentive and sustained interest.

I was personally very close to Edmond Jaloux and I retain a feeling of gratitude toward him, for, of all my critics, he and Charles Du Bos unquestionably showed the greatest understanding of my work. It was his great merit to perceive in my plays a close kinship between my own interests, indeed between my spiritual yearnings, and his own. In fact, I now reproach myself for not having carried out a project that I had formed during the Second World War, while living in the Corrèze, to devote a lengthy study to his fictional work. I had told him about my plan, and he looked forward to it with delight.

Cosmopolitanism, it cannot be sufficiently emphasized, was his most salient trait, and it permeated his work, as it characterized his personality. The essays and reviews in European and American literature that he contributed to *Les Nouvelles Littéraires* mark him as a man of broad cultivation and extraordinary perceptiveness. This worldly outlook

v

in the son of a provincial milieu — he was a native of Marseilles and born of French parents — is in many ways more remarkable than the universality of Charles Du Bos, who no doubt owed his cosmopolitanism to his mixed ancestry, part English and part French.

I am inclined to believe that the literary influences which Jaloux underwent were first and foremost foreign influences, despite the undoubted kinship that exists between Henri de Régnier's novels and his own early works, and despite a possible relationship with the fiction of René Boylesve. One of the most obvious of these influences is unquestionably that of Henry James. First among my friends and acquaintances after World War I, Jaloux urged me to read *Portrait of a Lady, The Aspern Papers* and *What Maisie Knew*. In connection with these foreign influences a great many other writers need to be mentioned. Amongst the Russians, first and foremost Turgenev, primarily the author of *First Love* and *Dimitri Rudine;* of Scandinavian literature Jacobsen's *Niels Lyhne*, Ibsen's later plays, and quite probably the work of Strindberg. The impact of German Romanticism upon him was no less strong. Thus we can detect the influence of Hoffmann's *Fantastic Tales*, which he read as a very young man, in all likelihood that of Novalis, and in a more evident way the effect of Jean Paul's *Titan* and *Quintus Fixlein*.

Nor must we lose sight of the fact that Edmond Jaloux was receptive to all kinds of poetry, and particularly to symbolist poetry, and that he loved painting, even the most modernistic, and music as well.

One wonders, in fact, whether Jaloux was not to some extent victimized by the almost inordinate range of his culture, by the excessive diffuseness of his interests. In this respect, as in so many other things, one notices a striking contrast between Jaloux's unbounded universe and the world of François Mauriac which, in the last analysis, is so thoroughly localized.

Miss Rosenfeld admirably delineates Edmond Jaloux's evolution as a novelist from such early works as *Les Sang-*

sues and *L'Ecole des mariages*, which are clearly linked to the realistic novel of that period, to the works of his maturity and of the last period of his life. In this phase the primacy of the occult and the imperative need to expunge the frontiers between the visible and the invisible, to obliterate the barriers between the real and the ideal, become increasingly evident. It is superfluous here to retrace in detail these various literary stages, for they are aptly portrayed by Miss Rosenfeld in her work. To characterize each period, she draws on the novels that she regards as the most representative within an almost disconcertingly profuse production. I shall confine myself to quoting one sentence which, I believe, defines very accurately the significance of the uninterrupted search that is present in all of Jaloux's works, most of which are today almost unknown. "His evolution as a novelist involved a continuous quest for the essence of reality and a protracted effort to convey it in esthetic form."

I vividly remember my last meeting with Edmond Jaloux at Lutry, shortly after the Second World War. He had not yet returned to Paris, that was then in the throes of partisan conflicts, and to which he was to return shortly thereafter. He was then a rather lonely figure, despite a few rare friendships such as that of Jean-Louis Vaudoyer, who was to succeed him as a member of the *Académie française*, and my own. I cherish his memory. He succeeded in achieving the final reconciliation of life's many conflicting elements — a reconciliation that is my own lifelong aim. It is indeed with affection and with gratitude that I recall his striving toward that goal.

Gabriel Marcel, de l'Institut.

Paris, June 1971.

TABLE OF CONTENTS

PREFACE

The fiction of Edmond Jaloux has not thus far been the subject of a comprehensive study. To be sure, essays, critical studies and reviews, assessing either a single novel or some aspect of the author's work, have appeared in newspapers and periodicals at various stages of his career. But these scattered appraisals fail to place individual works or specific themes within the general framework of Jaloux's evolution as a novelist. It is true that two books of a general character have been devoted to him. However, Yanette Delétang-Tardif's *Edmond Jaloux* is the nostalgic recollection of a friendship, while the study of Jack Kolbert, *Edmond Jaloux et sa critique littéraire*, takes up almost exclusively his nonfictional work.

The numerous criticisms of Jaloux's work, dispersed over many journals, tend to represent him as an attractive, but minor literary figure. That estimate, however, is based only on unconnected appraisals. By tracing his evolution as a novelist, I am able to correct in this study the traditional estimate of Edmond Jaloux. The author's abundant fictional output over nearly half a century, and the recurrence in his work of certain themes, would have made it difficult, however, to discuss each individual novel without being unduly repetitious. I, therefore, chose to discuss only the novels that reveal original approaches and new techniques, and that seem most perfectly to typify the various phases in the literary evolution of Edmond Jaloux. In so doing, I have always tried to situate Jaloux's works against the larger background of the twentieth century. In this way, I have found it possible to add to our knowledge of a revolutionary period in French literature.

While this study was in preparation, I was fortunate to have had an opportunity of meeting with Madame Edmond Jaloux, as well as with some of the novelist's closest friends.

I wish to thank Madame Jaloux for giving me invaluable insights into the author's personality, and for casting light on the genesis of several of his works. It is a pleasure to acknowledge the help that M. Gabriel Marcel gave me in elucidating the last phases of Jaloux's career as a novelist. I wish, moreover, to pay tribute to the late Emile Henriot for his sympathetic concern, and more particularly for directing me to the *Bibliothèque littéraire Jacques Doucet*, which proved to be a mine of information on Edmond Jaloux's relationships with his literary friends.

In completing the present work, I have benefited greatly from the guidance and suggestions of the New York University Faculty Committee that directed the initial version of it as a dissertation. I am grateful to Professor Bernard Garniez for his many valuable criticisms, and to Professor Anna E. Balakian for giving me the benefit of her unrivaled knowledge of the Symbolist and Surrealist movements. Professor Wilmarth H. Starr made useful suggestions concerning the early periods of Edmond Jaloux's career. I owe Professor Michel Beaujour a great obligation for the patient care with which he read my manuscript, and for the wealth and the incisiveness of the comments that he made. Several of the discrepancies that my book contained and some of its shortcomings were erased thanks to their kindly criticism. For whatever inconsistencies and shortcomings still remain, I am, however, alone responsible.

A Fulbright Fellowship to Paris, awarded in 1959-1960 and renewed for the following year, made it possible for me to gather unpublished materials on the life and work of Edmond Jaloux at the *Bibliothèque de l'Arsenal* in Paris and at the *Bibliothèque Méjanes*, in Aix-en-Provence, and to consult with some of the author's relatives and friends. It is thanks to the Board of Foreign Scholarships, in Washington, D.C., and to the U.S. government, who awarded me that fellowship, that I was able to complete the present work.

Fort Wayne, August 1971 M.R.

EDMOND JALOUX:
THE EVOLUTION OF A NOVELIST

INTRODUCTION

While the man of genius invariably ushers in a new era, the talented writer reflects his own time as a rule. To the latter class belongs Edmond Jaloux, a versatile novelist with a magic pen.

Coming of an austere middle class family, Edmond Jaloux grew up in Marseilles during the last quarter of the nine-teenth century.[1] From this transitional period, so rich in in-novations, he acquired a versatility which defies attempts at hasty classification. The multiplicity of his interests, which caused him to dilute his talent, was to affect his success as a writer. The outline of his narratives tended to become blurred, hesitant, and the ensuing mistiness estranged him at length from his audience and his critics alike.[2] Although it seems unlikely that Jaloux's novels will move out of their present obscurity, his evolution from concrete realism to dreamlike fantasy throws some light on the literary trends and crosscurrents of his time.

In this study I would like to examine the various stages that led a factual realist to the realm of imagination and mysticism.

Referring mainly to Jaloux's early novels, Daniel-Rops, Emile Henriot and Gérard-Gailly have placed this writer among the great family of French realists. These critics emphasize his early affinity with Balzac, Maupassant, Boy-lesve and especially Bourget.[3] Though Jaloux's first works show traces of these influences, the resemblance is tem-porary and more apparent than real. The formal didacticism of Bourget, his rigid psychology soon give way to the search-ing manner of a novelist who identifies himself with his own characters. Likewise the conflict between the individual and society, which forms the core of Balzac's Human

1

Comedy and of Bourget's problem novels, is soon superseded in the works of Jaloux by an exclusive concern for the inner man.

More conscious of the individual than of society, of latent feelings than of dramatic effects, Edmond Jaloux is above all a fine observer of the human spirit. To account for his people's motives and impulses, he penetrates far into the obscure regions of the mind. Villains and heroes alike are painted with a keen sense of shading, the action proceeding directly from their own personality. The claims of self-hood, which Jaloux had supported since the beginning, soon estranged him from his early masters. He responded immediately to the fierce individualism of Gide. The exaltation of man, his disengagement from social ties, meant more to the author of *Les Sangsues* than the pseudoscientific theories of Balzac and Bourget.[4] But for the understanding of the human heart torn between the seduction of evil and the yearning for ideals, no author had a greater influence over Jaloux than Dostoevski. The long dialectic which the latter carried on between freedom and submission, thought and action, crime and punishment, reverberated in Jaloux's own work from *Le Démon de la vie* to *La Maison des rêves*.[5] To the great Russian novelist he owes much of his progress from incipient determinism to a restless mysticism.

Contemporary authors such as Mauriac and Duhamel considered Jaloux a dreamer whose personages are as light as the fleeting visions that supposedly fashioned them.[6] However this type of criticism makes short shrift of the author's real aim: to express through the life of his characters the old universal truths, the inexorable laws that govern mankind.

After the era of realism which extends for him from the turn of the century to about 1910, Edmond Jaloux entered a transitional stage beginning right after World War I and lasting about four years. During this interlude he was characterized as an escapist writer by Emile Henriot, Maurice Martin du Gard and other critics as well.[7] The label stuck and the novelist never quite recovered his original rank as a serious creator of living characters. No doubt he reacted against the positivism of his youth when he renounced actualities to suggest, like the symbolists, the mystery of an elusive past of ancient towns and castles, of magic lands and scenes. But most critics failed to see that, by evoking the inner world of the author, these poetical novels lead directly to his most characteristic literary phase: the period of mystical expression.

By stressing hidden traits rather than obvious ones, intuition instead of pure reason, symbolist art deepened the novelist's vision.[8] Gradually Edmond Jaloux turned his thoughts to the inner life of his characters; at times he penetrated below the threshold of their consciousness. In this work, I plan to demonstrate how the poetical language of Jaloux's transitional period changed into the flowing monologue of an introspective literature and how this phase gave way in turn to a mystical quest for transcendence. My position is that a comprehensive view of the novelist's development disproves the traditional image of Jaloux as a light and superficial writer.

Great movements follow one another like the endless succession of waves. Thus the symbolists, reacting against the excessive earthiness of naturalism, paved the way for the discoveries of the surrealists. This evolution, of which the works of Jaloux project a faithful if somewhat belated image, is the theme of our study.

Part I

THE MAN AND HIS TIME

CHAPTER I

THE PERIOD OF YOUTH AND OF APPRENTICESHIP,

1878-1903

The saying that the boy is father to the man applies particularly to Edmond Jaloux. Throughout his life Jaloux remained faithful to the ideals of his formative years, and continued to express the outlook and prejudices of the milieu from which he sprang. In fact, it was precisely such an adherence to the outworn patterns of his youth which would later alienate him from the main literary and philosophical currents of his own time. Similarly his estrangement from the contemporary scene accounts for his eventual loss of interest in the society novel which he had cultivated assiduously before the First World War. This feeling of isolation would drive him gradually into a world of mystery and phantasy. Therein lies the significance of Edmond Jaloux's identity as a novelist, and therein lies also the reason for his relative neglect by the literary critics, a neglect from which he deserves to be redeemed. In order to understand Jaloux's position as a writer, it is necessary, therefore, to reconstruct the principal stages of his literary career. Edmond Jaloux was born in Marseilles in 1878, the only child of Jules Jaloux and Léontine, née Sauvaire. The elder Jaloux, an employee at the customhouse of the Marseilles harbor, and a man of limited vision and interests, belonged to a conservative bourgeois family in which there ran a deep strain of piety: two of his great-uncles were vicars-general in neighboring dioceses and four of his sisters became nuns.[1] Mme Jaloux, on the other hand, surpassed her husband in social refinement and literary interests. She belonged to a family whose mem-

7

bers were enterprising, and imbued with a real spirit of adventure. Léontine's mother, for example, had made a pilgrimage to Jerusalem while one of her brothers, who later became consul of France in Fiume, had joined Ernest Renan in his celebrated journey to the Holy Land in 1860-1861. Another brother established himself as a businessman in Russia.[2]

Among Edmond's clearest recollections of youth are his periodic visits to old and secluded relatives. These early contacts with a traditional household gave the boy his first impressions of bourgeois and provincial life. It was during these visits that he overheard arguments concerning family properties, wills and inheritances — subjects which were to form the main theme of his early novels. From his maternal uncle who had traveled to the Far East, the lad heard stories of the Orient which kindled his imagination.[3] By reading fairy tales to him, Léontine Sauvaire also stimulated her son's tendency to dream. Steeped in an atmosphere which favored the development of his poetic qualities, Edmond was fascinated by two titles he saw in a bookshop: Hoffmann's *Contes fantastiques* and Edgar Allan Poe's *Contes extraordinaires*.[4] These were the first books that he purchased, and their power to bring to life the most fantastic scenes was to exercise a profound influence on Jaloux's later novels.

During the late 1880's, however, when Jaloux began to discover the world of literature, naturalism was still the predominant movement. But it had reached the crest of a wave that was about to fall. A sign of the crisis appeared in a growing disaffection within the movement itself. For the naturalists' emphasis upon the coarse and material aspects of life was beginning to come under attack by Zola's erstwhile followers.[5] Maupassant himself now sensed the limitations of the realism that he had practiced throughout his younger years, as may be seen in *Le Horla*, a short story he wrote in 1887 and which communicates man's terror before the unknown. Similarly J. K. Huysmans, who started as a naturalist also, later dissociated himself from that movement turning his back on the sordid realities to create a universe of new and artificial sensations in *A Rebours*. Through the experiments of des Esseintes, the hero of that novel, the author called attention to Stéphane Mallarmé, prophet of an impending esthetic revolution.

At the same time poets like Maurice Maeterlinck and Paul Verlaine stirred their contemporaries with fresh images and musical rhythms which suggested the mystery of an enchanted world. These innovators presently supplanted the naturalists as the guides and inspirers of the new generation.

Edmond Jaloux was introduced to symbolist poetry through *l'Echo de la Semaine*, a Marseilles weekly paper. He was drawn at once to the new poetry, as he read in rapid succession Mallarmé's *Vers et Prose*, Vielé-Griffin's *Les Cygnes*, Henri de Régnier's *Tel qu'en songe* and a selection from Verlaine's verse. ". . . je fus ébloui par cette musique savante, cette richesse verbale, ces vers inouïs dont chacun pouvait s'isoler comme un vocable nouveau, à travers lequel apparaissait une lumière fulgurante," he recalled.[6] The young Jaloux was also reading Huysmans' *A Rebours*, in which he discovered the prototype of the decadent poet.

With its reliance on the magic of words to evoke the beauty of a transcendent universe, symbolism epitomized the period's weariness of common reality as well as its quest for renovation. Jaloux saw in that movement an exciting adventure, a road to the splendid world of imagination.[7] He was introduced, moreover, to such writers as Charles Péguy and Marcel Proust through the *Revue Blanche* to which he subscribed in 1893.[8]

From 1891 to 1893 Edmond Jaloux was a student at the Lycée Thiers in Marseilles. The emphasis on factual knowledge discouraged the young dreamer; he balked at the routine of drills and rote learning. Moreover his protected upbringing in the quiet and sheltered atmosphere of the family left him unprepared for the harshness of school life.

9

He hated the group, its insidious power, its oppression of the weak. A persistent cough that he contracted during the summer of 1893, and the fear that he was threatened by tuberculosis compelled him to withdraw from school. Presently he returned to the warm and familiar surroundings of his childhood. But the malice he had observed among certain types at school was to influence his vision of human nature.[9]

During the next seven years, young Jaloux was confined to his home. That span of time, which extended from his fifteenth to his twenty-second year, proved to be the crucial period of his development as an introspective and thoughtful person. Deprived of friendships and of outdoor life, Edmond began to seek satisfaction in an inner world of magic and fantasy. "Je me faisais peu à peu à une existence qui tendait à s'épancher dans une représentation de la vie, et non dans la vie elle-même," he recalled.[10] He also lived in the fictional realm of the theater and of the novel, ranging from the Greek dramatists to Shakespeare, from Dickens to Balzac.[11]

Summer, however, brought a welcome respite from that sedentary existence. During July and August, Edmond Jaloux would roam through the environs of Aix and admire the luminosity of the Provençal countryside, the purity of the colors at dusk, and the glistening of the crystalline mountains against the sky. He now began to take down impressions of nature: these were Edmond's earliest attempts at literary composition.[12] With the faith and the confidence of youth, he decided to become a poet. His mother encouraged him in that ambition. "Mes rêves, mes goûts réels, si précis déjà, mes premières lectures, mon ambition de devenir un poète, mes mélancolies, je lui dévoilai tout cela avec ce bonheur que l'on éprouve à sortir enfin de cette immense solitude morale qu'est l'enfance."[13]

Two short pieces which Jaloux wrote in 1895, Le domaine sentimental, a novel, and a poem En robe feuille-morte reveal his ingrained romanticism, as well as a wistful, melancholy temperament. While the novel related the fantastic adventures of a dreamy adolescent, Jaloux's poem reflected the musical rhythm of the symbolists. His verse, like theirs, reveals the quest for new and unusual harmonies. In 1896, Jaloux published his poem as the introductory piece of a collection entitled *Une âme d'automne*. He dedicated each one to some individual author whose work had recently inspired him. He thus became acquainted with such foremost literary figures as Mallarmé, André Gide, Henri de Régnier, and began to exchange a regular correspondence with them.[14]

No sooner had Jaloux gained a reputation in Marseilles as a poet than other southern writers and artists began to flock to his room on the rue des Tonneliers making it the headquarters of their literary gatherings. Jaloux's familiarity with the great writers of classical and romantic literature, as well as his cordiality and unaffected manner, quickly won him the friendship of such young Marseilles intellectuals as Francis de Miomandre, Albert Erlande, Théodore Lascaris, Joachim Gasquet, Gilbert de Voisins. These esthetes lived in an imaginary world of beauty that was nourished by their admiration of Watteau's ethereal vision, Gérard de Nerval's dreamlike phantasies, and Baudelaire's exotic mirage.[15]

The unexpected appearance of André Gide in their midst in May 1896, created a real sensation. "Si quelque météore, à la fois fulgurant et fabuleux, eût éclaté dans la pièce, je n'eusse pas été plus ébloui," remembered Jaloux.[16] Though still relatively unknown, the author of *Les Cahiers d'André Walter, Le Voyage d'Urien* and *Paludes* impressed the Marseilles group, for they recognized him as one of the new masters of French letters.[17] With his vast knowledge of world literature and his original insights, Gide spoke eloquently about Dostoevski, Thomas Hardy, Emily Brontë and Knut Hamsun. His enthusiasm proved contagious: Jaloux in turn began to discover these authors. He was fascinated by the subtle interplay of good and evil in Dostoevski's closed world. He never forgot the poetical vision of

11

Wuthering Heights or the sense of doom that pervades Hardy's stark narratives.[18]

But in their search for new modes of expression, Edmond Jaloux's literary circle was drawn more closely to French symbolism than to any of these great foreign novelists. The effort of the symbolists to evoke their peculiar dream world, to remain aloof from daily events and to attain new harmonies gave their poetry an almost magic character. Of all the symbolists, Mallarmé was the most revered and influential figure with the Marseilles group. "Il m'est presque impossible de dire ce que Mallarmé fut pour nous, (en 1896)," wrote Francis de Miomandre, "quand, à Marseille, où nous faisions une espèce de société avec Edmond Jaloux, Albert Erlande, Théodore Lascaris, Henri Roberty, Gilbert de Voisins et quelques autres, les vers du mystérieux poëte circulaient de l'un à l'autre, pour notre éblouissement unanime. . . . La raison de ce culte que nous avions, que nous n'avons cessé d'avoir, c'était, à notre insu peut-être, et venu du fond de notre *psyché,* le respect que nous inspirait un homme qui s'était, entièrement et sans réserve aucune, consacré à la poésie."[19]

Analogy and metaphor, the hallmark of Mallarmé's poetry, likewise permeated the works of the English romanticists. Jaloux and his friends now turned to Shelley and Keats to satisfy their longing for evocative imagery and perfect musical harmonies.[20] They also discovered Shakespeare whose creation of a world at once seething with reality and with fantasy moved them to the core. They loved above all the poet, the author of dreamlike and farcical comedies.[21] Thus they began to single out imagination as the most trustworthy guide to literary creation.

That romantic attitude fashioned their image of the major French novelists of the nineteenth century. Balzac, whom the realists had counted among their own, became a hero to the Marseilles literary circle, a mystic and creator of a fantastic world. The young men also admired Flaubert's power to evoke distant horizons and vanished civilizations, as in *Salammbô*. The macabre imagery of *La Tentation de saint Antoine* and the lavish oriental atmosphere of *Hérodias* fascinated them. Even in their discussions of Zola, Daudet and Maupassant, they emphasized the visionary and subjective elements of these authors.[22]

The esoteric character of these literary debates and their escapist tendencies were bound, however, to prove inadequate as a philosophy of life, particularly to a young man approaching the age of twenty. In the spring of 1897, as Edmond Jaloux was groping toward a more personal credo than these discussions offered, he received a copy of *Les Nourritures terrestres* from André Gide. The poetic vision of Africa and of Normandy glorified not only earthly joys, but also the liberation from crippling restraints and false standards. Gide's lyrical evocation of Algeria was a call to adventure, an injunction to seek one's own destiny. The story of a quest and a rebirth marked in fact the artist's break with the closed world of symbolism.[23] Gide's hymn to life had a tonic effect on the young southerner who immediately recognized the book's originality as well as its therapeutic value. "J'ai lu *Les Nourritures terrestres* dans une de ces époques confuses et troubles où l'on s'enlise dans la tristesse, entre la crainte du futur, le regret de l'autrefois, et le dégoût du présent," he confessed to his friend, "tout ce qui s'était amassé en moi de révolte vitale contre ma stagnation se réveilla. Vous m'avez mené vers la vie, vers la nature et l'amour."[24] From *Les Nourritures terrestres* Jaloux thus derived a fresh outlook; what moved him particularly was the fervor Gide brought to his art and to nature's infinite manifestations of life.

Presently, several French writers strove to escape from the artificial atmosphere of literary coteries and attempted to renew the source of their inspiration through a direct communication with nature. Jaloux, as we saw, also craved renewal. But his sedentary existence and the bookishness which he had cultivated in Marseilles made it difficult for him to absorb the freshness of the countryside. Nevertheless

13

when Francis de Miomandre and Albert Erlande visited him in 1897 at Saint-Loup, a seaside resort on the Mediterranean, their conversations were free from the intellectualism that characterized their discussions in the southern metropolis.[25] Like Gide they now began to move away from the rarefied atmosphere of the symbolists and to emphasize a spontaneous appreciation of nature. This new movement, which was soon represented by a few experimental journals in France and in Belgium, came to be known as "naturisme."[26]

During that year — 1897 — Saint-Georges de Bouhélier expressed the new climate of opinion when he ridiculed the excessive refinements of symbolism, and counseled a more direct approach to literature.[27] Unlike Mallarmé who saw nature's manifestations mainly as symbols of an invisible reality, Francis Jammes, Paul Fort, and Paul Claudel attempted to suggest in all their sensuousness the color, the scent, the very texture of the countryside. As a cofounder with Paul Fort of the review, *Livre d'Art,* Jaloux was a participant in the activities of that movement.[28]

Jaloux and his friends now decided to found a review of their own. Having heatedly debated editorial policy, the Marseilles circle brought out the first issue of *Méditerranéenne* in the fall of 1898, which among other pieces, contained poems by Francis Vielé-Griffin, Henri de Régnier and the Belgian symbolist Georges Rodenbach.[29] Throughout the next year, the new journal served as a medium for the literary experiments of the young group. As is usual with such undertakings, the review ceased publication after one year due to lack of financial backing and continual bickering among the editors.[30]

The failure of that venture did not, however, destroy the coherence of the Marseilles literary circle, nor did it deter Jaloux from completing a novel, *L'Agonie de l'amour.* In that work he denied the romantic ideal of love and thus expressed the *fin-de-siècle* disenchantment of his own generation. The passages which he read struck a deep chord, for his friends recognized their own feelings in these pages, and

14

they consequently urged him to send his manuscript to *Mercure de France.* In 1899, the twenty-one-year-old author watched with mixed joy and concern the appearance of the novel that started his long and checkered career as a man of letters.[31]

By 1900 the founders of *Méditerranéenne* had dispersed, a few having even left Europe. The isolation in which Jaloux now found himself and the stifling restrictions of his provincial milieu oppressed him.[32] Occasional visits of André Gide to Marseilles relieved the uneventfulness of that existence. The author of *Les Nourritures terrestres* also offered his younger colleague some excellent advice, emphasizing above all the need for directness and simplicity in the description of character and in the treatment of situation.[33] Though Jaloux tried to apply these principles of composition when he wrote *Les Sangsues* in 1901, the novel itself, with its minute description of provincial pettiness and greed, is too typical of the late nineteenth century *roman de moeurs* to have come under the influence of Gide's new ideas.

One year after the appearance of *Les Sangsues,* Gide's *l'Immoraliste* was published in *Mercure de France.* Jaloux was deeply impressed by the novelty of its theme and by the philosophy which it advanced. Gide's ethical system advocated the realization of the individual through a long and arduous search for his most genuine self. This ethic, which combined personal discipline with a restless curiosity for life's many possibilities, brought to Jaloux the message of renewal which he so ardently sought. For he felt like a prisoner behind the thick walls of conventions which society erects, and the gradual liberation of Gide's impetuous hero from all social ties spoke of an invigorating experience. "Je me sens tout près de Michel," wrote Jaloux, "sa curiosité, je la reconnais, c'est la mienne, trop de ses paroles et de ses sentiments correspond en moi pour que je le limite et m'effraye de lui. Combien de jeunes gens d'aujourd'hui en diront-ils autant? S'ils sont sincères, beaucoup, je crois. 'Nous sommes au seuil d'une époque de culture nouvelle.' "[34]

Protée, a short story Jaloux wrote in 1906, reflects the exploratory aspects of this philosophy, as it presents a hero who gradually discovers himself by experiencing diverse and contrasting adventures. However this fervor for life in all its forms did not harmonize with the bleak, deterministic tone of Jaloux's realistic novels. If his early *romans de moeurs* do not show any traces of Gide's dynamic vision, this absence is due to the fact that the younger author looked to his elder, at first, as a spiritual guide rather than as a man of letters.[35] When he wrote about his southern milieu, therefore, he was influenced by the regional novelists who had instilled in him the notion that man should be viewed in relation to his social and geographic environment.

Ferdinand Fabre impressed the young provincial with his vivid accounts of life in the Cévennes mountains. He appreciated the authentic flavor of his country scenes; he was fascinated by the descriptions of the Cévenols' thirst for material security. René Boylesve's subtle analysis of human feelings and his impressionistic sketches of Touraine appealed even more to the Marseilles youth, for he loved the delicate portraits as well as the misty landscapes. Moreover, from the author of *La Becquée* he learned to see, beneath the placid surface of small towns, the hidden drama of lowly and obscure lives. The colorful and evocative vignettes of Fabre and Boylesve spoke to the young southerner of his own provincial childhood, of the greedy bourgeoisie that surrounded him.

Jaloux's next book *L'Ecole des mariages,* expressed the artist's aversion for his prosaic milieu. For in that work, he satirized the scheming and sordid transactions by which bourgeois families contracted their marriages in order to rise in society. During this period, Jaloux was subduing his romantic nature and striving to master the art of description. Not prepared as yet to articulate his own vision of life, he found the practice of minute observation, of adherence to visible reality conducive to better craftsmanship. But the concrete description of the petty bourgeois, their clothes, their houses, their carefully planned schemes, proved a heavy task. Jaloux soon began to feel the sterility of this external realism, the need to slough off outworn styles.

The consciousness that he was adrift in his province filled him with a desire to leave the balmy indolence of his Mediterranean climate and to seek wider horizons. Speaking of himself and of a friend, Jaloux thus expressed that hope:

> Il nous fallait commencer notre course, trouver nos juges et nos témoins, nos détracteurs, s'il le fallait, mais enfin une résistance en face de nous. Nous demeurions sur place, inconnus de tous et de nous-mêmes, comme des faons qui n'ont pas encore couru, des lionceaux qui n'ont pas encore chassé![36]

That period, around 1903, marked the beginning of Jaloux's protracted search for the novel form that would enable him to convey the atmosphere of his inner world.

CHAPTER II

THE MAKING OF THE NOVELIST, 1904-1949

At the turn of the century, when Jaloux was longing to try his talents, all roads led to Paris. Famed for its elegance and intellectual vitality, Paris seemed the mecca of all true artists. It was the city where poets, painters and musicians freely discussed questions of style and form; it was also the home of literary *salons* and cabarets. Jaloux was eager to participate in the life of the capital. He wanted, as we saw, to compete with other aspiring authors, and to find his own identity as a writer.

On his arrival in Paris during the spring of 1904, he was met by André Gide who welcomed his southern friend by inviting him to his home and by introducing him to *La Closerie des lilas,* a favorite haunt of avant-garde artists. Within a few weeks, however, Jaloux realized that he must make his way independently, by his own efforts and experiences. He decided to move to a room in Montmartre, then still the hub of artistic bohemia. Rowdy and unconventional, this motley crowd of students, poets, and jesters met in the smoky atmosphere of Montmartre's cabarets, where they loudly proclaimed their contempt for the bourgeois establishment. Jaloux never tired of watching the colorful ways and picturesqueness of these out-and-out bohemians, but he rarely took part in their discussions, being less turbulent and having to struggle, moreover, against the inevitable obstacles of an impecunious young writer. A feeling of loneliness often gripped him as he wandered about the city's silent neighborhoods. He suffered at first from the anonvmity of the capital, the indifference of publishers, the difficulty of

18

gaining admission in a closed and stratified society. It was not long, however, before he began to appreciate the stimulating atmosphere of the great city.[1]

While revisiting his old friends who had preceded him to the capital, Edmond Jaloux also made new contacts in the literary cafés of the left bank, and he soon participated in the controversies that pitted traditionalist against modernist.[2] His deeper nature had always drawn him toward the imaginative life, though this propensity as well as the influence of symbolism touched only his poetry at first. His cultivation of realism in the novels of manners, we saw, served the purpose of a literary apprenticeship. "L'époque où nous vivions était soumise à un réalisme sévère; l'esthétique de Flaubert et de Maupassant pesait sur nous et il fallait d'abord faire l'expérience du réalisme et de ses méthodes ou trouvailles avant de penser à lui échapper."[3] In Paris he discovered some new perspectives that would loosen the grip of realism. He was particularly drawn to Paul Fort, who transmuted all of life's experiences into an exuberant and ingenious poetry, as well as to the dreamlike imagery of Saint-Pol-Roux's verse.

Jaloux's relationships with these poets and other writers gradually broke down his feelings of isolation in the capital. He was also gaining access to a few Parisian literary salons whose fashionable assemblages captivated him at first. But if Jaloux appreciated the society of drawing rooms, he loved Paris above all for the freedom from bourgeois restrictions which it conferred, for the intensity of its intellectual life and the prestige with which it endowed all creative activities.[4] In spite of its realistic strain, *Le Jeune homme au masque*, a penetrating analysis of the young men about town whom Jaloux encountered on his visits to the salons, reflects the fascination of the Marseilles novelist with Paris during those first months of his stay, while he discovered the radiance, the gloom, the countless and pervasive moods of the capital. The appearance of this novel in *Les Essais*, a

Paris literary periodical, won him the lifelong friendship of its editor, Jean-Louis Vaudoyer.[5]

To this period also belongs *Le Reste est silence*, a novel of manners, which reveals the fusion of realistic and symbolist elements. This work contains a poetic evocation of Jaloux's own youth, transposed into the reminiscences of a young man from Marseilles, who relies on sense impressions, on the visual and creative memory to recapture the world of his childhood. When the novel was published three years later, it won him the *Prix Fémina* and a wide circle of admirers.

Another Marseilles friend with whom Jaloux renewed his acquaintance in Paris was Auguste Gilbert de Voisins, a student of Asiatic civilization and society, and the author of several novels of adventure.[6] Gilbert de Voisins was connected to a group of naval officers and explorers who had lived in Indochina and in other parts of the Far East. At meetings of that circle in the home of his friend, Edmond Jaloux was introduced to such religious and ethical systems as Hinduism and Taoism, from which he began to derive an interest in Eastern mysticism. "La pensée asiatique était au fond de nous comme une flamme douce et pure," Jaloux recalled, and his affinity for the Orient increased as he gradually turned to the occult.[7] Beneath that exoticism, however, lay a yearning to lift the pall of habit, to see the world with the fresh and wondering gaze of childhood.

The interest shown by Jaloux's generation in Eastern art and philosophy reflected a weariness with imitative realism, and a search for beauty which characterized artistic Paris at the turn of the nineteenth century. This cult of the beautiful manifested itself in the assiduousness with which Pierre Louÿs strove for an immaculate style, in the efforts of Edgar Degas to capture the elegant movement of the dance, and in Claude Debussy's quest for the rendering of pure tones and liquid harmonies. It appeared also in the flowering of the decorative arts.[8] Jaloux himself was fond of all kinds of tapestries and *objets d'art*, and he collected

20

them in his apartment on the rue de Valois, near the Palais-Royal.

We saw that the circle of Jaloux's acquaintances widened, as he was introduced in 1906 to various literary salons. Many of these gatherings were tightly knit coteries, which admitted only members of the conservative upper class. At the home of René Boylesve he met a number of these traditionalists. He particularly cultivated the friendships of Henry Bordeaux and René Bazin, who were both regional novelists, and both defenders of a hierarchic social order.[9] But Jaloux also encountered men of his own generation and of esthetic temperament: Emile Henriot, a young novelist later to turn literary critic, the poet Paul Drouot, Charles Du Bos, an eloquent and perceptive essayist, and the youthful Mauriac.[10] Having spent their formative years during the symbolist period, these younger men were more receptive than their elders to new literary and philosophical currents, and also more cosmopolitan in their tastes. They nevertheless embodied the way of life and the prepossessions of the relatively stable era that preceded the outbreak of the First World War.

The receptions of Mme Muhlfeld were more fashionable than Boylesve's staid evenings. There the great names of the world of letters, art, science and politics mingled with pretty women, celebrated for their charm and witty conversation. Jaloux, who later recognized the vanity and emptiness of these society gatherings, was fascinated at first by a world whose remoteness had endowed it with unusual glamour and prestige. He would always remember Anna de Noailles as she appeared to him in the days of her youth, and his first encounters with Henri de Régnier, Paul Valéry and other writers whom he had admired as a solitary dreamer in Marseilles.[11] These social reunions were enlivened by the wit and sparkling erudition of Anatole France, the disabused remarks of Paul Hervieu, the humorous tone of Henri de Régnier.[12]

More important however than these literary relations,

21

were Jaloux's contacts with the women he met in the salons. Invariably they felt drawn to him by his vibrant personality and by the genuineness of his feelings. Coming of age about 1900, Jaloux belonged to an esthetic period that tended to idealize women.[13] Among the two who would influence him most, one of them, Germaine Koïré, later became his wife; the other, the gifted Yanette Delétang-Tardif, would find her way to the man's heart.[14] But in the first decade of this century when he began to lead a mundane existence, the friendship and confidences of these society women already had given him an understanding of the instinctive female heart. Presently he incorporated these insights in such novels as *Le Démon de la vie* (1908), and *l'Éventail de crêpe* (1911) which explore the passions and irrational impulses of the characters while recapturing the social atmosphere of Paris on the eve of the First World War.[15]

During these years Edmond Jaloux recognized in Jean-Louis Vaudoyer a kindred spirit, for they were equally fervent admirers of authors who upheld the values of traditionalism. They both revered Maurice Barrès, praised the lyrical prose with which the author of *La Colline inspirée* expressed his attachment to the ancestral soil, and emulated his ardent nationalism in a mutual dislike of Captain Dreyfus and his liberal allies.[16] Jaloux and Vaudoyer similarly admired Paul Bourget, whose novels epitomized the *fin-de-siècle* reaction against a stifling positivism and the period's search for spiritual values. Jaloux, moreover, shared Bourget's hostility to the demagogic tendencies of democracy, as well as his belief that a hierarchic social order constituted the best antidote against the abuses of a competitive society. The author of *Le Reste est silence* was drawn to these representatives of nineteenth century conservatism by the remembrance of the world of his youth, as well as by temperament. Almost instinctively, he clung to the style of life and to the system of values of a world that was dying out.[17]

An era marked by social stability and firm regional attachments was indeed drawing to a close. In 1905, the various

22

Socialist parties, reacting against the fervent nationalism of the Conservative Coalition, merged under the leadership of Jean Jaurès to fight the entrenched power of the bourgeoisie. By seeking to control the means of production and to reapportion the distribution of wealth, the Left hoped to close the gap that separated the middle class from the masses.[18] But a sign of the period's social unrest appeared most ominously in the Syndicalist movement of Georges Sorel. For his belief in the violent overthrow of the capitalist system was translated into action by a series of prolonged strikes attesting to the deep cleavage between the bourgeoisie and the proletariat.[19] The latter's tendency to identify with labor movements in other countries, helped to create a spirit of solidarity among the workers which transcended political frontiers and which razed the barriers of provincialism.

Great changes were likewise taking place in the realm of art and letters. Having lost confidence in the value of representational art, the avant-garde poets and painters of the early twentieth century experimented with new forms and techniques in the hope of discovering a more authentic reality. Their disenchantment with the age-old traditions of Western art, explains the enthusiasm for Negro sculptures when they first arrived in Paris from Africa around 1907. Characterized by solid masses, deep notches and projecting angles, these wooden carvings expressed the statuesqueness of the human figure with a simplicity that touched the innate sense of rhythm and movement. The stark beauty emanating from these bare forms influenced such painters as Braque and Picasso to reduce all shapes to their geometric components and to rearrange them in such a way as to transport the viewer from his limited world into the magic realm of artistic timelessness.[20]

Closely associated with these adventurous seekers of new and unbounded vistas are the major poets of this period: Guillaume Apollinaire and Max Jacob. Their startling associations, jumbled images and terse refrains correspond to the

23

fragmented, dislocated and angular paintings of the cubists. By placing themselves in a state of mind particularly receptive to the automatic and verbal flow of their subconscious, these poets succeeded in creating an imaginary world that clearly foreshadowed the dreamlike visions of the surrealists. An effort to transcend visible reality likewise typified the novel of that period. Convinced that the methods of nineteenth century realism were now outworn, a number of young novelists, such as Marcel Proust, Alain-Fournier, Gide as well as Edmond Jaloux, began to develop a deeper insight into the world about them than the traditional regional novel, with its objective scrutiny of physical or social phenomena, had allowed. For they strove above all to capture the elusive moods of an ever changing and inner reality. To reach the true self with its hidden recesses and conflicting emotions, these authors resorted to intuition, dreams and analogies. But in trying to render this complex reality they came up against the limitations of a hackneyed novel form, and saw the need for renovation.[21]

The musical world of this period also underwent a profound transformation. By fusing the graphic, musical and dramatic arts, Sergei Diaghilev was able to create a spectacular new ballet. Its repertory included such pieces as Stravinsky's *Rite of Spring* and the *Firebird Suite*, which introduced new harmonies with their atonal scales. It also included Borodin's *Prince Igor*, whose tumultuous enchantment fascinated the younger generation. Edmond Jaloux and his friends loved these performances. For them the pageantry of Diaghilev's ballets would forever incarnate the excitement and youthful fervor of artistic Paris on the eve of the First World War.[22]

During that period, Henri de Régnier, together with his young admirers Edmond Jaloux, Jean-Louis Vaudover and Emile Henriot, also spent some unforgettable days absorbing the color and the splendor of Venice. To these votaries of art, the mysterious palaces, the antique shops filled with glassware and carved furniture, the animated piazzas all

24

spoke of the light and romantic atmosphere of a bygone age.[23] Thus, the city of the Doges worked on them like an incantation, and Edmond Jaloux for one, caught its nostalgia in *l'Alcyone,* one of the last of his society novels.

Though Jaloux's horizons were expanding, he remained a traditionalist at heart. His incurable nostalgia, his yearning to recapture the past link him to such writers as Proust and Alain-Fournier. However his respect for tradition and his faith in the continuity of literature, explain the unfaltering loyalty to such men as Bourget, Boylesve and Henri de Régnier. The world in which Jaloux was born and bred — the safe, predictable and stratified world of the 1880's — was dying out. Would a man of the nineteenth century, such as he, reveal a sufficient depth of insight to foresee the crisis that confronted his generation, or to articulate the larger issues of his time? Such a question should be raised in connection with the outbreak of World War I, for that global conflict ushered in a new age of violence and instability.

The war in fact underscored the failure of the principles and the values by which European society had lived throughout the nineteenth century. The harrowing experience of trench warfare proved a tough school which transformed many of its participants and witnesses, and Edmond Jaloux was no exception. As a hospital attendant, he saw the devastating effect of war upon men.[24] That experience ultimately gave rise to an encroaching fatalism which later would appear in his novels. At the time however, Edmond Jaloux, in a movement of revulsion turned away from a reality which seemed too harsh to bear.

Two novels, *Fumées dans la campagne* and *l'Incertaine,* which appeared in 1918, are far removed from the anxieties of war. The first work deals with the return of a young man to Aix-en-Provence. It is a lyrical evocation of Jaloux's own past. The other, a novel of imagination with symbolist overtones, recounts the story of an adventurous girl who refuses to accept the constraints of a proper bourgeois marriage. Both of these books convey a poetical quality that would characterize certain French novels in the immediate postwar years. Disheartened by the spiritual void, the materialism that he sensed, Jaloux created in his novels a visionary existence whereby he hoped to redeem the ugly reality of a world he inwardly rejected.[25] Thus *Au-dessus de la ville,* written in 1919, a novel of psychological analysis in which each of the protagonists incarnates some fundamental concept, reveals the contrast between two modes of life: the aristocratic traditionalism of the later nineteenth century, and the new crudeness of the postwar world.

Withdrawal from society led to a growing interest in the deeper reaches of human consciousness. In this connection, Jaloux owes a great deal to such novelists as Turgenev and Henry James. From these writers he learned new techniques, particularly the ability to recapture fleeting impressions and reconstruct hidden thought processes, as well as devise more subtle characterization of persons.[26] Jaloux's understanding of human nature was further developed by his discovery of *A la recherche du temps perdu.*[27] With its exhaustive analysis of people's real motives, of their capacity to revive the past through fortuitous sensations and of their evolution in the course of time, Proust's novel leads to a contemplation of the real self. Emphasizing the inner life of his characters and their infinite complexity, Jaloux now revealed in three books, *La Fin d'un beau jour, L'Escalier d'or* and *Les Profondeurs de la mer,* written in the early 1920's, the impact of these various influences. For he had now forsaken the conventional society novel of his early years, and was instead studying men and women in conflict with their own time and struggling to resolve their inner contradictions.

The postwar years were Edmond Jaloux's most creative period as a novelist and as a critic of literature as well. From 1922 onward, he was a regular contributor to *Les Nouvelles Littéraires* for which he reviewed a wide range of books, representing nearly all of the European literatures. Through his weekly column "L'Esprit des Livres", he kept

26

abreast of the main literary and ideological developments of his time, and also made himself the advocate of figures and movements that were striving for recognition. His articles also encouraged the popularization of foreign authors within France.[28]

Two novels, *Le Rayon dans le brouillard* and *L'Alcyone*, written in 1924 and 1925, reflect Jaloux's mood of disillusionment with the postwar world. At odds with the rough and turbulent spirit of a new age, the protagonists tend to retire within themselves and to live in the realm of thought. But instead of finding solace in this contemplative life, a weariness comes over them. For these characters represent the individual's inevitable solitude in an oppressive environment, and his search for a path to personal salvation. In their struggle to remain what they are, these personages recall some of Mauriac's own people — tormented figures as Thérèse Desqueyroux and Jean Peloueyres who prefer ostracism and disgrace than to lose their personal identity. Jaloux's growing alienation from his time estranged him from the mainstream of postwar thought and drove him increasingly into experimentation with the literature of fantasy.

That return to the world of imagination aroused Jaloux's interest in German romanticism. In the middle twenties he began to appreciate writers such as Jean Paul Richter, Novalis, Arnim, Tieck and Heine.[29] He particularly admired their ability to unite sharpness of observation with an infinitely rich and creative imagination. He praised these German authors' pantheism, which enabled them to fathom some of life's mysteries, and thus briefly transcend the limitations of the human condition.[30] Jaloux's reading of Poe and Hoffmann, as a youth, foreshadowed that later preoccupation with mysticism. But as mature writer he was better able to appreciate the visionary qualities of German Romanticism than during his formative years.

Jaloux, however, owed his true initiation into the language of myths and dreams to his friends, the poet Rainer Maria Rilke and the playwright Hugo von Hofmannsthal, who

27

sensed by intuition the invisible relationships between man and nature.[31] Like these prophets of the inner life who deplored the passing of an age and the death of individualism, Jaloux was pained by the soulless conformity which he felt all around him. Instinctively he sought refuge in the poetical universe of these Austrian mystics. In three novels: *O Toi que j'eusse aimée, Soleils disparus* and *Laetitia,* written between 1926 and 1929, he dramatizes his own predicament by portraying young intellectuals unable to come to grips with a reality they fear. But the leading protagonists of these books are too self-centered to arrive at real moments of truth. Incapable of detaching themselves from their little private worlds, and thus reaching a communion with the universe, these characters merely seal their own doom by their withdrawal from the society of their fellow men.

Standing outside the mainstream of literary production, Jaloux was turning more and more to his English contemporaries. He was among the first to champion the cause of James Joyce, whose *Ulysses* he extolled because it minutely reconstructed the inner workings of the human mind. He felt an even closer kinship to Virginia Woolf, for her novels revealed a new version of the stream-of-consciousness technique, more subtle and refined than the one initiated by the Dublin novelist.[32] Influenced by *Mrs. Dalloway* and *The Waves,* Jaloux gradually abandoned the framework of the traditional novel, supplanted it with a transcription of incipient thoughts and feelings, and also suggested associations of ideas. Jaloux acknowledged his debt to the new English novel in *Au Pays du roman,* a collection of essays in praise of the literary and psychological innovations made by recent writers of the British Isles.

In 1932 Jaloux published *La Balance Faussée.* That novel, the story of an insane girl, illustrates the author's newly developed interest in the subconscious. Having analyzed the dread visions and morbid jealousies of a demented person, Jaloux was demonstrating the persistence, even in his own day, of myths first worked out by the Greek dramatists — myths which exemplified the despair of those who cannot triumph, for all their striving, over the obstinacy of an evil fate.[33]

While Jaloux now confined himself to describing man's elemental drives, a new school of French novelists hammered out in the fire of war and revolution a modern version of the heroic life. André Malraux plunged into the social upheaval of his time and advocated a firm commitment to some unselfish cause. Saint-Exupéry exalted physical danger, particularly the flyer's lonely battle with the elements. Other writers however, such as Céline and Georges Bernanos, attempted to convey the somber and chaotic atmosphere of a world in ferment. But Jaloux, as a true conservative, eschewed these burning issues of his own time and remained faithful to the prewar ideal of individualism.[34]

Three novels, *La Grenade mordue*, *La Chute d'Icare* and *L'Egarée*, written between 1933 and 1938, revive ancient Greek themes in a contemporary setting, respectively the old myths of Proserpina and of Icarus, and also the story of Perseus and Andromeda. However, while the heroes of Malraux and Saint-Exupéry struggle against fate and seek to conquer it, the characters of Jaloux's later novels are invariably defeated by a cruel destiny. These introspective and vacillating beings stand in sharp contrast to the dynamic and willful heroes of the novel of adventure and of social protest.

Having reached his maturity in an age that practiced art for art's sake, Jaloux clung throughout his lifetime to the conceptions of his youth. He loathed the directness of the literature of *l'entre-deux-guerres* that reflected the brutal and violent tendencies of contemporary life. In the concise history of the Symbolist movement which Jaloux wrote in 1936 for an anniversary volume, he showed that he regarded the world of art as the only haven from the period's chronic unrest and as the sole remedy against the continual disintegration of life.[35]

That year, Edmond Jaloux became a member of the

Académie française, filling the chair left vacant by the death of Paul Bourget. In his inaugural speech, Jaloux again underscored the continuity in French literature of the traditional emphasis on the interrelation between the individual and society.[36]

The outbreak of war in 1939 did not bring about any fundamental change in Jaloux's conception of life and literature. Though he sympathized with the new Pétain government in 1940, he retired to Lutry, on the Lake Leman, where he had spent many a previous summer.[37] In the stillness of his mountain retreat, he chose as a new theme for his novels the connection between man and his natural environment. Influenced by the literature of French speaking Switzerland, through which there ran the perennial theme of man's fundamental loneliness and his inability to communicate with others, Jaloux created solitary and eccentric characters in search of themselves, as in the novel *Le Pouvoir des choses, Le Culte secret* and *Le Pays des fantômes,* written during and after the Second World War.[38]

"La Pêche aux flambeaux," the last novel which Jaloux wrote, shows that his career as an author had run its full course. In this final and still unpublished work, Jaloux expressed his mystical vision of an unlimited dream world in which the characters, freed from the limitations of space and time, can partake of different existences. Having shaken off the yoke of the visible world, Jaloux also gave up the contrivance of a fixed plot, thus altogether disregarding the traditional sequences of time, the usual relationships to places, and the habitual identifications of individual characters with specific persons.[39] Doubtless, Jaloux's own closeness to nature in his mountain retreat helped to detach him from all worldly concerns, and thus made him the more conscious of the hidden reality that permeates all aspects of life.

The liberation of France enabled Jaloux to return to Paris. He now divided his time between Lutry and the French capital, where he resumed his activities as a literary critic, and where he participated, on the conservative side, in the post-war controversies that pitted the adherents of the new republican government against the erstwhile sympathizers of the Vichy regime.[40] But he would not long survive these implacable political hatreds. He died at Lutry in the summer of 1949.[41] That event reminded the men of his generation who outlived him that an era in French literature had now drawn to a close.

Part II

THE REALIST

CHAPTER III

THE REGIONAL NOVELS OF MANNERS

The provincial artist who aspires to become a writer often begins by choosing subjects related to his native region. The more isolated he feels from the outside world, the more likely he is to find inspiration in the familiar setting of his province. Rooted in Provence and steeped in its cultural heritage, Jaloux thus started out as a regionalist: the restlessness of Marseilles' bourgeoisie, its volubility, its exuberance and intrigues constitutes the central theme of his early novels. Moreover, Jaloux's journalistic activities on behalf of an autonomous literature in Southern France testify to his strong feeling for regionalism in those early years spent in Marseilles and in Aix-en-Provence.[1]

This movement had started in the second half of the nineteenth century when a number of writers reacted against the excessive centralization of the State and its policy of linguistic uniformity by reasserting the value of their indigenous dialects and literatures.[2] The provincial novel of manners, which grew out of this regional renaissance, owed its descriptive technique to the exact and unembellished vision of such artists as Courbet and Champfleury. Their minute portrayals of different localities and social classes, contributed greatly to the development of an artistic regionalism in France.[3] That genre thrived mostly in those provinces which maintained their ancient customs and traditions.

For example Ferdinand Fabre so thoroughly understood the life of his Cévennes mountains that he communicated his love of the land and the rugged spirit of its inhabitants in such novels as *Les Courbezon* and *Mon Oncle Célestin*.[4]

Similarly, Eugène Le Roy who knew the very stones of Périgord, renders with unusual acuity the sounds, colors and smells of his native region. In the remote villages of the Vosges mountains, Emile Erckmann and Alexandre Chatrian undertook to present jointly the life of simple farmers, artisans and winegrowers. Against the background of Napoleonic wars, their artless tales bring out the picturesque and evocative customs of the people of Alsace.[5]

Still largely agrarian and impervious to outside influences, the province with its distinctive character and fierce individualism offered the novelist a variety of subjects. In its constricted atmosphere, passions often flared up, the more so, because they were repressed by the parochial attitudes and the scrutiny of prying neighbors. Excessive supervision bred reticence. Beneath the placid surface of small towns, tempests raged. A wide gulf thus separated truth from appearances, and it is this secret reality which captured the imagination of such regional novelists as Fabre and Boylesve.[5a] Having read their books at an impressionable age, Jaloux was stamped by realism. He began to observe surroundings and to probe people's motives; he imbibed the principle that characters should be portrayed both as individuals and as members of their social group.[6]

In his apprenticeship as a realist, Jaloux owed much to the *Comédie humaine* whose characters seemed so true to life that he constantly recognized them among his contemporaries. Balzac's fascination with houses as revealers of people and his creation of a vast, generic society influenced the beginner, particularly in his early novels, where the evocation of a teeming city and the reappearance of familiar characters suggest the whirl of an organic community.

Important though this reading proved to be in molding Jaloux's style, his intimate knowledge of Marseilles looms larger in his development as a writer. For he was immersed since childhood in the Mediterranean atmosphere: Marseilles' prosperous harbor, its streets swarming with people, its parks, trees and deserted neighborhoods had become so deeply engraved in his mind that he could conjure up these sites at will. Through weekly visits to old and sedentary relatives, we saw, he had gained an insight into the provincial bourgeoisie, its traditionalism, its frugality, its unquenchable thirst for material possessions.[7]

Stimulated by these experiences, he wanted to portray the manners and the psychology of his class. He had suffered in the intensely commercial atmosphere of Marseilles from a feeling of spiritual exile – a feeling which explains his irritation against the philistines.[8] Jaloux's vehemence contrasts with the dispassionate tone of Fabre and Erckmann-Chatrian. Even more than his predecessors, the southerner had seen how grasping bourgeois society can be. Undoubtedly his sense of loneliness, his painful awakening to realities account for the stinging sarcasm of his early works.

Between 1901 and 1903 Jaloux wrote *Les Sangsues* and *L'Ecole des mariages*, two novels linked by a unity of tone and subject. They both accentuate the seamy side of bourgeois life; they describe the provincial milieu so graphically as to recall the pictorial style of Flaubert and Maupassant.

Les Sangsues, a bleak and sinister tale of a man ruined by the family he supports, first appeared serially in *Le Mercure de France*. Though published as a book in 1904, the original version goes back to 1901.[9] Jaloux dedicated his novel to Gide, whom he greatly admired, but whose advice he followed gingerly and with regard to style, rather than form or content. Thus Jaloux waited three years before sending his manuscript to Plon, emended his text, reorganized entire chapters and altered paragraphs. The smooth language of the finished work gives an impression of ease which belies the effort that went into the writing of that novel. The clear style corresponds to a neatness of structure, for the various threads of the novel's minor themes are woven so skillfully into the larger tapestry that the general effect is one of utmost clarity.

The novel in many ways is indeed a typical *roman de moeurs*, a grim story of family intrigue for money, after the manner of Balzac and Boylesve. A gentle and kindly ecclesiastic who runs a school for boys has taken under his wing his widowed sister, Mme Pioutte, and her two daughters, Cécile and Virginie. Only a small part of their late father's wealth remained to them, for he had squandered his money in the course of a dissipated life. Their brother, Charles, is following in the footsteps of his father. Living in Paris, ostensibly to study art, he keeps a mistress, a former model, at his family's expense. He prevails upon his mother to send him additional funds. Mme Pioutte is passionately devoted to her son. She is willing to go to any lengths to gratify his every whim. In order to help Charles liquidate his debts, Mme Pioutte pressures her brother, Abbé Barbaroux, into providing a handsome dowry for her daughter Cécile, a fact that she carefully conceals from the girl. Her mother now coerces her into an unwanted marriage, with the argument that she is a burden on her uncle. Cécile gets married, while Charles pockets his sister's dowry. When the young woman discovers her mother's stratagem, she is mortified to the core. Cécile is determined to create a scandal that will discredit her entire family. Through extravagant spending, she manages to ruin her husband, who then attempts to recoup himself through fraudulent practices. Money alone can hush up the family scandal, and once more the priest turns out to be the reluctant provider.

While the home is racked with fighting, Father Barbaroux's position becomes the object of a fierce rivalry between two members of his teaching staff. Augulanty, the school's ambitious bursar, seeks to take over the establishment by ousting the clergyman. Mathenot, a teacher at the school, also covets the headmastership. The two men struggle in a desperate contest for supremacy. Neither, however, succeeds in fulfilling his ambitions, but their rivalry has undermined the reputation of the school. Abbé Barbaroux finally discovers the plot to deprive him of his office, and he dies a sorely disillusioned man.

During his initial stage, Jaloux's way of describing with minute accuracy people's faces, clothing and houses, marks him as a late realist after the manner of Boylesve and René Bazin. The novelist then relies on objective and concrete evidence to characterize his personages, for the world of natural phenomena constitutes the only guide to truth. Restricted by that positivistic view, the novelist proceeds somewhat like the historian, collecting documents to revive a shadowy past or to bring its blurred figures into clear focus.

This deliberate fusion of fiction and history may be seen in the portrayal of Father Barbaroux. To give his hero the appearance of having actually lived, Jaloux narrates his youth before opening up the family drama, stressing his role as a soldier in the Franco-Prussian War. In conformity with the realist's graphic vision, Jaloux tries to heighten the impression of authenticity by describing in great detail the man's physical appearance. "L'abbé Barbaroux ... avait le front haut, sous une flottante chevelure grise ... , le nez osseux et envahissant; les joues creusées, la bouche grande et mince, peu de lèvres, un menton de galoche et quelque chose d'ascétique dans toute sa figure austère et labourée de rides."[10] But excessive detail dims the outline of Barbaroux's features, while the novelist's concreteness blinds him to the slow evolution of a man's character.

Having found truth in the religious life, Abbé Barbaroux wholly devotes himself to teaching, to sustaining his widowed sister and her children. He is indeed a kind of saint endowed with such extraordinary charity and patience as to seem almost superhuman, and on that account, neither recognizable as a real person, nor truly convincing. Nearly all his life, Barbaroux retains the reassuring optimism of his youth, and his discovery of evil coincides with the dramatic necessity of the novel, rather than with the gradual transformation of a disillusioned man. Overwhelmed like certain characters of Flaubert and Maupassant, by the shock of a cruel revelation, Father Barbaroux dies shortly after seeing his ideals and his lifework reduced to ashes.

Yet, it is only during this brief moment of revelation, when he becomes aware of the social turpitude, when he suffers, doubts and questions that we feel the inner tumult of a defeated man groping towards an answer. "J'ai été le centre de mille intrigues.... Moi, qui ne voulais que le bien, j'ai, par le seul fait d'avoir agi, répandu le mal autour de moi. Il y a donc quelque chose d'empoisonné dans l'air pour que les meilleures intentions produisent des crimes?"[11] Until his eyes are opened, however, by this sudden and belated vision, Barbaroux lived in a benign world of illusion; his blindness to the harsh realities explains the immobility of his character.[12] A generous and even tempered man day after day, his uniform behavior lacks the motion and the complexity of life — a complexity that the realist with his photographic vision, fails to suggest.

The portrait of the sly bursar, Félix Augulanty, reveals the objective point of view, which the novelist still adhered to, his acceptance of the positivist principle that environment and appearance are unmistakable signs of character. Thus Félix's anemic face suggests a cunning and shifty person; even as his room, with its faded wallpaper, its rickety furniture and slovenliness speak of the man's devious and hypocritical ways. In his passion to succeed, moreover, the bursar recalls the unscrupulous social climbers of Balzac's *Comédie humaine*.

Despite the persistence of this nineteenth century point of view, Jaloux now tries to discern, under external appearances, the character's inner struggles and conflicts. While the novelist illuminates only the conscious and rational thoughts of Abbé Barbaroux, he now also conveys the rage and the confusion of an ambitious man spurned by the young lady on whom he counted to lift him out of mediocrity. The reader hears him vent all his anger and resentment:

—Ah! elle me refuse! Ah! elle est sûre de ne jamais m'aimer et de ne jamais m'épouser!

Je suis un trop petit sire pour elle! On ne réduira donc pas l'effroyable fierté de tous ces riches, puisqu'ils la conservent même quand ils sont ruinés.... [13]

Of lowly origin and oppressed by a feeling of inferiority, Augulanty senses condescension and contempt in the most innocuous words and gestures. Through flattery he tries to work his way up; his vehement outbursts, when his plans fail, enable the reader to catch a glimpse of the man's real nature.

Jaloux was hampered, however, in his attempt to convey these inner tumults by the restricted vision of his early realism. Unable to evoke the flow of images, thoughts and feelings that constitute a person's semiconscious life, he dramatizes the character's most crucial moments — moments during which a surge of emotion seems completely to paralyze the restraining power of reason. Augulanty gives himself away, for instance, in his reaction to defeat, whose sting brings out the ruffian and makes him behave savagely. ". . . maintenant il mordait; sa vraie nature, si longtemps comprimée, reprenait le dessus, et la brute reparaissait." [14] Fretful and envious, always suspecting others of scheming against him, Augulanty seems more alive than the saintly and guileless priest. For the latter tends to become fixed in his unfaltering zeal as a religious and humanitarian person, whereas in the case of the former it is the insecurity of the upstart that the novelist tries to portray.

But these probings into the mind are too fragmentary, as we saw, to provide a vision in depth, or to offset the artificial impression resulting from the novelist's tendency to plan his character's every action and to pull all the strings. For all his plausibility, Augulanty seems fictitious, a character manipulated by an omniscient novelist to bring the action to a head. Although the reader senses the inner turmoil of a warped personality, he sees the ambitious

41

bursar from the author's objective point of view, and this external vision accounts for the absence of any vibrant or emotional quality in the portrait.

Augulanty's rival for the school's executive post is a stern and dour priest. Setting himself up as an example of moral righteousness, Mathenot is the very antithesis of Barbaroux. Like most professional reformers, he sees evil lurking behind every human face. Because of his fanatical zeal, Mathenot completely misses his goal. His reiterated diatribes against women and his suspicion of life's earthly joys wean his students away from the religious life.[15]

In conformity with the naturalistic doctrine, character and appearance coincide. Tall and gaunt, Mathenot instills fear. The meanness of his nature is reflected in a face disfigured by pockmarks and in a pair of dark eyes which squint with the false stare of the bigot. His voice has the shrill sound of a crow. Even his awkward gestures bear witness to a spiteful nature. "Rien n'était plus antipathique à voir que ce grand diable sombre, chafouin, avec sa large figure vulgaire, convertie en passoire par la petite vérole. Sa voix rauque et sourde, ses yeux défiants, sournois, soupçonneux, la maladresse de ses gestes heurtés, tout avait chez lui le même caractère désagréable."[16] A weird cross between the Spanish inquisitor and the Puritan reformer, Mathenot stands out more as a typical zealot than as an individual in flesh and blood. In the restrictive environment of the province his missionary zeal finds little outlet. His schemes founder on the rock of his inflexible nature. The villain proves in the end to be a fool.

Like these crudely drawn figures who appear either as saints or villains, the women with their clearly defined traits and predictable conduct also reflect the viewpoint of a stereotyped naturalism. For, what remains in these portraits, of Zola's lurid scenes of the working classes, trapped in the cycle of poverty and degradation, is the recurring parallelism between man and beast. The naturalistic tendency to bring out the animal in human beings obviously subsists in the portrait of Mme Pioutte, the scheming widow, whom Jaloux pictures as the living embodiment of evil. Her withered and emaciated face, her cruelty and greed invariably call to mind the gruesome image of a bird of prey. To her trusting brother who painfully discovers that she has cheated and robbed him time after time, "... il parut tout à coup ... que Gaudentie (Pioutte), avec son oeil gris, devenu cruel et aigu, son grand nez crochu, son long cou nu et ridé, ressemblait à un vautour et qu'elle était prête à fondre sur lui."[17]

The method of making a character stand out by showing the devastating effects of a single passion is one which Jaloux owes to Balzac.[18] Thus it is with a mad attachment, the kind of devotion Père Goriot lavishes on his daughters, that Mme Pioutte seeks to gratify the whims of her dissolute and spendthrift son. "... pour qu'il soit heureux, je serais capable de tout!" she screams to l'abbé Barbaroux, "je balayerais les rues pour le voir sourire, j'assassinerais pour qu'il se paye un plaisir."[19] She does not struggle against this emotion, for it has all the virulence of an incurable disease. Like so many of Balzac's protagonists, Mme Pioutte tyrannizes those around her, because she in turn is completely possessed and dominated by a single passion.

Of Balzac's fresh and vibrant realism, however, the young novelist has appropriated certain techniques, not the power to breathe life into people. For all her feverish activity, Mme Pioutte appears as a stock character of satiric comedy, the typical shrew or schemer. Nor does her wild passion for her son reveal much about the real human being. For the minute realist, concerned mainly with facts, saw her maternal infatuation not as a clue to temperament, but as a means of setting in motion an intricate plot. To a large extent, it is this prearranged action which determines and explains the behavior of the main characters. Always preoccupied in devising some plan, and always able to choose the right moment for developing her schemes, Mme Pioutte seems endowed with almost prophetic foresight. Her ability to calculate everything in advance hastens events as well as the novel's outcome, but this prescience gives her a mechanical appearance. The spontaneity as well as the tragedy of a fortuitous and unpredictable life are missing here.

Mme Pioutte's daughter, Cécile, an intense and emotional young woman who inwardly rebels against her hidebound bourgeois milieu, emerges as the most convincing character of the novel. Like the others, however, she cannot elude the crippling effect of a rigid plot, and its influence explains why the passionate, lively creature of the beginning finally becomes a soulless robot. Before the inevitable ending, however, the heroine's reactions are so real, that her vibrant personality compels admiration. In accordance with realistic techniques, the novelist illuminates the hidden and sensual traits of the young woman by showing her in a state of crisis during which we perceive the storm raging within. "—Regarde-moi donc! Regarde mes épaules, mes bras, ma gorge! Ne suis-je pas belle?" she cries out to her mother, "Ah! passer ses plus belles années de force, de jeunesse et de beauté, dans cet ennui, dans cette inaction, dans cette torpeur! Ne rien sentir, ne rien voir, ne rien éprouver, n'avoir pas une occasion où goûter la vie!"[20] Beneath the particular grievances that she voices, one can feel the rebelliousness of suppressed instincts, of the real self against the encroachments of social conformity.

To revenge herself, Cécile dreams up a scheme: she will drive her husband to bankruptcy and thus force her uncle to pay off the cost of averting the disgrace of a public scandal. This fiendish plotting hardly accords with the spontaneous character of a young woman thirsty for life. But in order to bring the drama more quickly to a head, Cécile must exploit in her turn the generosity of the kind and unsuspecting priest. As the narrative progresses towards its inexorable ending, Cécile hardens, until she too becomes an extorter, a leech whose greed precipitates the final tragedy. Reduced at the end to the level of a puppet,

Cécile has lost not only the ardor of her first appearance, but the vital human quality to react in a personal way to unforeseen events. Father Barbaroux's sudden agony brings out the cold egoist Cécile has now become as she sees in her uncle's approaching death the convenient cancellation of her debt to him. While her callous indifference to another's suffering manifestly reveals the stifling effect of a mean and constricted environment on an impetuous personality, her maliciousness seems hard to believe. Once more the determinist's bleak outlook and his contrived plots necessitate the radical transformation of a personage, in this instance, from an unpredictable, lively girl into a calculating shrew.

Les Sangsues offers the gruesome picture of a family despoiling its breadwinner. In *L'Ecole des mariages*, the novelist shows a whole town pitted against an individual. Characters reappearing from one novel to the next, the rise of the parvenus, the decline of a prominent family, all heighten the impression of movement of an organic and complex society. "Déjà avant la vingtième année," recalled Francis de Miomandre "(Jaloux) édifiait de vastes constructions . . . où toute une société est passée en revue."[21] Influenced by Balzac and Zola, Jaloux adopted some of their sociological concerns.

At the turn of the century many a middle-class marriage was still arranged by a go-between. Jaloux loathed the incongruous unions patched together for social considerations only. He had witnessed the suffering caused by ill-assorted marriages and regarded matchmaking as the principal social evil.[22] Variations on this theme show that Jaloux was preoccupied with this question which, in his eyes, epitomized the falsehood of human existence. Thus *Les Sangsues* shows a misalliance leading to tragedy, while *L'Ecole des mariages* illustrates the calamitous effect of social intrigue in bringing about a marriage.

Although the regional novelists' descriptions of the provincial bourgeoisie had inspired Jaloux at the outset, he relied

45

mainly on his own observations of Marseilles society to convey the quality of behavior and conversational tone of his characters. As Miomandre aptly remarked: "Son étude constante n'était pas livresque; elle se référait toujours à la vie même."[23] L'Ecole des mariages is based moreover on a local item that relates a domestic tragedy caused by the meddlesomeness of an officious clique.[24] By adding personal recollections to the theme of this real situation, Jaloux constructed a novel whose vividness and symmetry greatly enhance the dramatic impact.

Mme Guitton, the wife of a successful financier, draws Marseilles' fashionable world to her weekly receptions. The glitter of these parties reflects credit on the hostess. Wherever high society assembles, she is invited to come. But her star soon grows dim. The bell tolling for her husband's death signals her own downfall. The drawing room that had witnessed so many brilliant festivities, is now completely deserted. To restore her dilapidated estate, the widow embarks in a shady business. Whatever the cost, she must win back her place in the city's most exclusive circles. The indifference which her former guests now show, fills her with a longing to recapture her golden days.

Mme Guitton has known René Delville, the heir of an enormous fortune, since boyhood. For many years she turned over in her mind the thought of marrying her daughter Fanny to this young man. But he had his mind set on another girl, Edmée Diamanty. From her mother who died during her confinement, Edmée had inherited a frail constitution. Rumor had it that no more than her mother would she survive the labors of childbed. With the intuition of a woman, Mme Guitton sensed that Delville would never consider marrying her daughter as long as he had not satisfied his heart's desire. Although the schemer knew about the precarious state of Edmée's health, she does her utmost to bring about the wedding. A spurious medical certificate has been drawn up to mitigate the anxiety of Edmée's father and to vanquish his opposition. Mme Guitton also enlists the active support of the society women to facilitate meetings between the two young people. Her carefully worked out plans are beginning to yield results. The marriage between Edmée and Delville takes place and presently M. Diamanty's forebodings of impending doom come to pass. Edmée dies as she gives birth to a sickly child.

For a time the grief-stricken widower shuns all human contact. But after a dreary winter, he finds himself again making a circuit of the various social gatherings about town. Mme Guitton's hour has struck as she lures the young man into the meshes of her tangled designs. She throws into relief the resemblance between her daughter and Edmée, and she flatters him so skillfully that he finally succumbs to her blandishments. As Delville takes Fanny as his wife, Mme Guitton's dream of retrieving her social position comes true at last.

Although Jaloux's method of characterization is becoming more subtle, he is still restricted in his development as an artist by the pervasive influence of positivism, particularly by the principle that environment and heredity can explain all of human behavior. As in *Les Sangsues,* Jaloux continues to introduce his characters in a setting that presumably reveals their temperament and their way of life. Mme Guitton, for example, is first seen in a house whose faded luxury clearly indicates the dweller's own downfall. A few dishes of wrought silver and a carved mahogany table are vestiges, in this impoverished home, of a past opulence that is gone. The incongruous sight of ill-assorted and shoddy furniture also bespeaks her sudden fall from prosperity.[25]

To a large extent Mme Guitton and the heroine of *Les Sangsues,* Mme Pioutte, have similar personalities. In their determination to reach a certain goal, they both display a single-mindedness that borders on insanity. Neither hesitate to use other people as instrument of their designs. Moreover, their faults can be traced back to greedy ancestors, after the naturalistic doctrine of hereditary traits.

Yet in spite of these resemblances, Mme Guitton's portrait

is by no means a replica of the former. For the novelist now penetrates much further into the woman's character by illuminating her murky and twisted mind:

> . . . elle cherchait continuellement un refuge contre les souffrances et l'irritation que lui causaient le sentiment de sa déchéance et le spectacle de sa ruine. Tomber devant l'opinion d'autrui est une torture incessante pour celui qui a mis tout son bonheur dans cette opinion. Humiliée, saignant par toutes les blessures faites à son amour-propre; dévorée de jalousie, affolée par la vue du luxe et des dépenses de ses amies, Mme Guitton ne songeait qu'à prendre avec le mariage de Fanny une revanche qui serait aussi une vengeance.[26]

Jaloux's growing interest in the deeper motivations of life accounts for the slow build-up of events, which greatly overshadow their outcome. The character's mood, his peculiar traits, his outlook on life are brought into sharp focus, so as to put the reader in his place, thus giving him an impression of close contact.

But the novelist's external description of character subsists, for all his efforts to transcend visible reality, and this lingering concreteness explains why Mme Guitton fails to arouse any sympathy, in spite of her despair: ". . . quand elle sortait du salon d'une amie riche et triomphante, son désespoir d'être tombée si bas se transformait en frénésie. Un désir, effroyable de violence et de passion, la tourmentait et la déchirait. Elle voulait, coûte que coûte, retrouver son ancienne splendeur, et satisfaire les coûteuses exigences d'une vanité dévorante."[27] The novelist's factual account gives the character not soul or spirit, but forcefulness.

For lack of inwardness, the more tangible qualities of energy and cunning create an impression of extraordinary vitality. Mme Guitton works hard to gain admission into the city's most exclusive circles. She ingratiates herself with the most influential ladies in town and, by dint of sheer perseverance, manages to recapture something of her former glory. Having promoted the marriage of Delville and Edmée, and thus caused the hapless girl's death in childbed, Mme Guitton blames others for the crime which she has perpetrated. Whenever the subject of Edmée's death recurs in any conversation, the wily schemer reveals all of her acting talent. The shrill voice then assumes a doleful quality as she wails over the tragedy of her unwitting victim. But the pretense of sorrow is too transparent to be convincing. The casual rejoinder "... que voulez-vous? C'est la vie!" with which she punctuates the remarks of her guests, confirms once more her utter indifference.[28]

These evil ways do not stem from a fundamental weakness of character, as is the case with the heroine of *Les Sangsues*. Not a blind and irresistible passion, but an indomitable will to recoup her losses dictates all of Mme Guitton's acts. In a spirited conversation with her brother, she exhibits the extent of her self-knowledge. "Comme moi, tu es vil," she tells him, "comme moi, tu es bas, médiocre, mais tu as réussi et j'ai réussi, et le monde me saluera comme il te salue."[29] Wealth to her is synonymous with power and the urge to dominate becomes so thoroughly ingrained that she gets to be a victim of her own delusions.

These characterizations reveal the influence of nineteenth century regional fiction with its minute descriptions of external reality and its structured plots. The effect of its linear vision helps to explain why this otherwise powerful image remains frozen and two-dimensional. For Jaloux does not quite succeed, in his early *romans de moeurs,* in resolving the contradiction between the individual's own personality and the modalities of a positivism that envisaged the character as the inevitable product of his social and physical milieu.

As a regional novelist, moreover, Jaloux was particularly interested in the relationship between people and their class. Indeed, *L'Ecole des mariages* evokes the stirring movement

49

of a teeming city in such a way as to make society the focal point of the entire novel. By shifting his attention from the static environment of *Les Sangsues* to the coming and going of a whole society, Jaloux began in fact to loosen himself from the grip of his *fin-de-siècle* and provincial realism. For the method of copying the tangible world proved inadequate when it came to seizing the little social nuances, the tone and atmosphere of Marseilles' fashionable salons. Their presentation henceforth reveals a sharpening perception, the urge to look beyond restrictive, often misleading appearances. The novelist now interprets more than he describes, and this change of method underscores his awakening search for a more personal vision of reality.

Flashes of insight, imagination and humor begin to animate the people satirized in *L'Ecole des mariages* and to dispel the somberness of Jaloux's early realism. Despite an excess of minute detail, he now makes his society come alive by revealing, beneath the masks that men usually wear, the signs indicative of character and inner thought. Through his satire of Marseilles' bourgeoisie ring notes of personal resentment and of the artist's quest for the unvarnished truth.

For example, with a flair for comedy, Jaloux ridicules a crowd of carping women who regularly congregate in the homes of the newly rich Mmes Malval and Dampierre to satisfy their curiosity, to besmirch the reputation of their young acquaintances and disparage the poor. On gossip they live, and Jaloux, still a precisionist at heart, notes their every word. But instead of emphasizing what they say, it is their manner that he now brings out. "Mme Bergeon fait des mines et murmure des potins d'une voix angélique et flûtée. . . . Ils vivent comme des bêtes," she complacently remarks about the poor "avec une moue de mépris qu'aucune langue humaine ne saurait traduire."[30] Unwitting revelations of a character's deeper personality now loom larger in *L'Ecole des mariages*. Thus, in his struggle to convey a living reality, Jaloux gradually widened the scope of his vision.

As a young man, Jaloux saw that provincial people were wont to display a dogged stubbornness, whenever they decided to concentrate all their efforts on a single aim. As the critic Rachilde aptly remarked: "C'est en province qu'on a le temps d'ourdir les plus sombres drames; là on peut se servir de la complicité d'une ville."[31] Society undermining the individual's will until he is forced to give in; such is the meaning of the little drama being enacted in this provincial milieu by an old and firmly established community. With their taste for intrigue, Mme Guitton and her friends attempt to draw Delville and the sickly girl together. For they hope, through rumor and innuendo, to obtain the consent of Edmée's father for the fatal match.

When all his efforts to avert misfortune have failed, M. Diamanty feels so weary and defeated, that he offers no further resistance. Having lost his inner strength, he merely drifts along with the stream. Resignation takes the place of rebellion, and with it a soothing tranquillity apparently sets in. But the peaceful expression merely represents the calm before the storm. Edmée's untimely death elicits neither a gesture of despair, nor a word of regret from the disconsolate father. In the funeral procession his thoughts wander for a moment to the memory of his late wife. Presently the images of mother and daughter become blurred. Coming on top of a string of woes, this loss proves too grievous for him to bear. The coordinating threads endowing a person with vitality suddenly give way, and leave the old man a mere shadow of his former self. "Ce petit vieillard à visage d'ivoire, à regard terne et lent, devenait une dépouille d'humanité. . . ."[32] With an understanding culled from personal experience, Jaloux brings all his sympathy to bear on this touching narrative which may be read as a parable of life.

Next to the moving and subtly drawn portrait of her father, Edmée Diamanty does not cut much of a figure. While the impression of pallidness may be attributed in part to the girl's weak health, it is the novelist's return to the minute descriptions of *Les Sangsues* that accounts for the general blandness of her character. Jaloux's portrait of Edmée, which represents every feature of her face, every detail of her dress, leaves paradoxically only a vague and blurred image in the reader's mind even as the typical characteristics of the fictional heroines of that period, such as the slender figure and the pale face, contribute to a sense of indefiniteness.

Elle était grande, svelte, élancée. . . . Son cou frêle et long supportait une figure pâle, un peu maigre, très fine, aux traits comme estompés. Autour de son front et de ses tempes translucides, où les dessins des veines semblaient en relief, sa chevelure d'or cendré bouffait avec une coquetterie négligente. Ses paupières longues dévoilaient des prunelles grises d'une grande douceur où il régnait de la tristesse. . . . Un cerne les entourait, qui n'était point brun, mais bleui et d'un ton de meurtrissure extrêmement délicat.[33]

Similarly, the precise description of her room fails to give an idea of the dwelling's peculiar atmosphere, and it therefore tells very little about the life of the young woman. By seeing Edmée's personality reflected in the objects and the arrangement of her house, Jaloux oversimplifies the portrait, and gives it a stereotyped look. As if he sensed the insufficiency of this method, the novelist penetrates occasionally below external appearances and shows that the girl's egoism coexists with her fundamentally kindhearted nature. But in this picture, which reveals a return to the concreteness of his beginnings, Jaloux fails to convey the fluidity of a changing personality and thus the movement of life itself.

The interplay of light and shade in the drawing of René Delville, on the other hand, makes this portrait a fascinating study in contrast. With a keen sense of reality, the novelist opposes the young man's apparent self-assurance and his actual weakness. In accordance with the naturalistic outlook, Jaloux solves the riddle of René's dual personality by relating his formative years. An orphan since the age of five, young Delville never conquered the child's instinctive dread of loneliness. Entrusted to the care of a foster parent, his carefree and pampered childhood merely accentuated his insecurity, and this upbringing made him incapable afterwards of overcoming any disappointments. The first blow he suffers fills him with a profound sense of personal inadequacy.[34] Probing Delville's motives, the novelist elucidates his mercurial character. René's irresolution stems from his innate contradictions. Though aware of his inner weakness, Delville lacks the will to transform himself. For want of perseverance, his noble resolutions never materialize.

Jaloux believed that a man's attitude towards women invariably reflects his character. Delville is fully conscious that he dominates Edmée. Moreover, and more significantly, he derives a secret pleasure from inflicting pain on the girl he loves: "Le visage en pleurs de la jeune fille lui donna je ne sais quelle joie voluptueuse."[35] Hints of René's fickleness, and frequent allusions to his unconscious sadism make this equivocal character stand out with unusual relief.

Keeping aloof from the crowd, Sunhary, one of René's friends, is the objective onlooker of this drama. One literary critic refers to this young man as the most fascinating character in the novel.[36] Yet to this writer Sunhary does not seem convincing. His arrogance is too obviously reminiscent of that turn-of-the-century sophisticated air which the literary dandies wore as a badge of distinction. Of this group André Beaunier has given the following description: "Autour de 1900, il y eut en France une jeunesse dorée chez qui l'amour n'était pas en faveur. La dépravation de l'esprit lui parut élégante; la perversité mentale et morale à la mode."[37] Sunhary shares the snobbishness of these young decadents as well as their artificial intellectualism. In his desire to infer the laws of human behavior and to develop a universal theory of conduct, he appears as a rather fictitious being, one who combines the scientific passion of Bourget's Disciple with the intuition of Ménalque, Gide's prophetic and influential hero. Looking down on the world with haughty condescendence, he is never drawn into a real-life situation. His urbane irony thus proves irksome in the end.

Sunhary's voluntary aloofness and his analytic mind facilitate his discovery of the complex and secret motives which inspire human actions. As the detached observer, he often voices the author's own opinions. But his attempt to grasp reality through cold observation clearly illustrates the limitations of Jaloux's initial and objective point of view. In a revealing passage at the end of the book, this view is concisely summed up:

L'homme n'est point isolé et libre dans le vaste monde, il communique avec tous, et tous le dirigent. Il n'y a pas de faits uniques, sans motifs et sans conséquences. Les êtres sont des marionnettes que des fils secrets relient entre elles.[38]

It is this initial social determinism that prevents Jaloux from developing independent characters. Mere pawns in the game of life, they have no choice other than submission to their fate. Whenever Jaloux breaks away from his determinism — this confirms my concept of conditioned behavior — his men and women become real and convincing. But the novelist's continued adherence to a philosophical and literary doctrine whose vitality was in fact dying out, accounts for the uniform pattern and less than subtle interpretation of the characters of his early work.

CHAPTER IV

TRANSITION FROM THE SOCIETY NOVEL TO THE NOVEL OF THE INDIVIDUAL

The arrival of Edmond Jaloux in Paris in 1904 inaugurated a new phase of his literary activity. He was feeling increasingly constricted, we saw, by his adherence to a realism which merely described the social and external aspects of human behavior. To friends whom he met in the capital at *La Closerie des lilas,* such as Francis de Miomandre and Gilbert de Voisins, Jaloux expressed a desire to portray the inner man: "Tantôt avec l'un, tantôt avec l'autre, j'échangeais des vues sur le moyen de donner au monde intérieur que chacun porte en soi, . . . une raison plastique de vivre, une convenance nouvelle."[1] For his interest was shifting from the concrete world of society to the invisible flow of man's inner life. The static picture of a selfish bourgeoisie was being supplanted by a complex and dynamic portrayal of the individual's own reality.

The two principal novels of this transitional period are *Le Démon de la vie* and *Le Reste est silence,* which appeared in 1908 and 1909 respectively. Traces of Jaloux's early realism, however, are still evident, for instance in the graphic description of Parisian society in the former novel, and in the evocation of Marseilles in the latter work. But the change of focus from the mundane to the spiritual life explains why the physical action becomes simpler, why it no longer determines the behavior of the characters.

Moreover the author's minute description of faces, typical of his early style, has given way to bold and revealing drawings of the personality. For it is not an exact likeness

55

that the novelist seeks, but the power to suggest character by means of a few expressive traits:

Le grand salon communiquait avec un petit boudoir japonais. Peu de lumières. Simone était assise dans un fauteuil; Jacques se tenait sur un pouf, et la regardait d'un oeil câlin, où passait parfois un éclair coupant comme un coup de faux, puis il reprenait son air bénin, doucereux, langoureux. Robert regarda tout à coup ses mains. Ce n'étaient pas les mains fines, délicates, fuselées de l'homme qu'il paraissait être, elles étaient larges, rudes, la paume carrée, les doigts épais, habituées à prendre et à garder, et elles démentaient la douceur veloutée de ces yeux bleus, la délicatesse de ces cheveux bouclés, toute la séduction de ce bel homme fin.[2]

In this sketch which contrasts the aristocratic looks of a man and his real nature, Jaloux reveals the ambiguousness of visible reality as a clue to character.

Similarly his portraits of the female characters, though they still picture details of dress and appearance, no longer convey that sense of immobility which characterized the personages of Jaloux's early *romans de moeurs*:

Simone descendait d'un pas léger, petite, mince souple, la taille flexible. . . . Sa robe de dentelles blanches se fondait avec la pâleur de ses épaules frêles et de ses bras minces. Elle avait je ne sais quoi d'aérien, de flottant, de musical. Sa démarche avait un rythme, un ondoiement cadencé . . . elle avait la grâce d'un rayon animé, l'errante et mélancolique splendeur d'une étoile filante, que son éphémère destinée rend touchante comme un être vivant.[3]

The visible details in this portrait fade in importance beside such abstract qualities as frailty and sensitiveness which foreshadow the girl's premature death. To express these qualities, Jaloux no longer resorts to minute descriptions, but to poetical images and similes; the sparkling charm of the personage is compared to a ray of light, her brief and tragic fate to the swift passage of a shooting star. Presented through a kaleidoscope of changing images and points of view, the characters are no longer rigidly fixed; they come to life as the reader interprets their actions or identifies with their feelings. The evolution from photographic realism to impressionism and from reason to intuition comes to light, as we shall see, in *Le Démon de la vie* and *Le Reste est silence.*

Though the first-named work remains to some extent a society novel, whose action takes place in the Paris salons at the turn of the century, the bleak outlook of Jaloux's early work is giving way to a subtle and more complex vision of life. Influenced by Robert de Clausel, her proud brother who is a devotee of art, Simone, the leading character, likewise develops her esthetic sensibility, and thereby alienates her frivolous relatives. But she herself quickly rebels against her purely cerebral existence. For a while, she is in doubt as to which course to follow; she finally decides to return to her family's gay and mundane life. Soon she falls in love with the unscrupulous Jacques de Motheau, whom she has met at one of her mother's parties, and for some months carries on an affair with him. When Simone discovers that her lover has kept his former mistress, she sinks into despondency. Her brother, with his customary aloofness from all emotional involvements, sarcastically censures her conduct which he sees as a stigma on the family. Alone in her distress, and crushed by a double betrayal, Simone de Clausel takes her own life.

The novelist's conception of reality has turned inward, so that the feverish activities of society now form but a background for an incisive study of character. In his novels of introspection, Jaloux tells the story from the point of view of the characters themselves. He achieves this impression of coexistence with another by revealing the individual's emotions, particularly the tumult of feelings welling up in the mind and heart, after a cruel deception.

The more Jaloux emphasizes characterization, the less he delves into the manners and idiosyncrasies of the various social classes. Thus the novelist's description of a dinner party suggests the glib conversational tone, but not the spirit of Parisian society:

Tous éprouvaient cette sorte de gaieté montante, d'optimisme, de satisfaction de vivre que communique l'entrain d'un dîner. Chacun se plaisait et plaisait à autrui. Robert . . . répondait avec agrément à Mme La Mousse, qui lui confiait qu'elle était bien seule dans la vie et lui faisait des compliments détournés. Mme d'Angilbert s'amusait des potins de Ludovic d'Orson, Tancrède piaillait des mots féroces, des allusions cyniques, . . . Mme Norghèse écoutait les fadeurs que semblait transpirer le lymphatique Enguerrand Rivoyre du Pont; et chacun oubliait sa vie pour participer à une ivresse commune, factice, éphémère et charmante.[4]

Drawing rooms decorated in the characteristic manner of the eighteenth century, form a fitting background for the gatherings of that frivolous set.

Simone's meeting with Jacques is the highlight of *Le Démon de la vie.* He asks her to dance, and as he whirls her about with complete self-assurance, she feels greatly attracted to him. From the very beginning, de Motheau appears as an equivocal individual. Simone sees only his attractive aspect, and develops a genuine passion for him. Fully aware of the girl's affection, he cynically exploits her love. Jaloux's sharpened vision manifests itself in this incisive portrait of a dissembler, who readily adapts himself to all kinds of persons and circumstances. "Cet homme indifférent était habile à pénétrer chacun de ses interlocuteurs et à parler sa langue."[5] Accustomed to courting pretty women, de Motheau has a peremptory way with them that makes him irresistible. But in the end, as we saw, he betrays his true physiognomy: the scoundrel beneath the handsome looks. In this portrait in which appearance and reality disagree, the novelist reveals his growing skepticism of the visible world as a guide to truth as well as his search for new methods of characterization.

The novelist's attempt to penetrate the enigmatic faces of his characters appears more eloquently however in his moving portrait of Simone de Clausel. Jaloux has abandoned lengthy and minute descriptions of facial expression, clothing and houses that were his stock-in-trade in his early period of realism. He now sheds light on the fleeting but significant gestures that disclose the individual's true feelings:

(Simone) semblait inquiète et parlait nerveusement à son amie. Un moment où Robert se tournait vers elle, il vit son regard troublé se diriger vers Motheau et Mme La Mousse. Ce regard jaloux fit à Robert l'impression d'une coupure en plein coeur. Cela c'était encore une certitude ajoutée aux autres. . . . Tout à coup, comme n'y tenant plus, Simone se leva et alla vers Motheau et Mme La Mousse, au fond du salon. Robert n'entendit pas ce qu'ils disaient, mais ils riaient tous les trois. De quoi? Ce rire était une feinte. . . .[6]

As the portrait appears through the anxious and tormented vision of the girl's brother, it acquires the vibrancy of living experience.

The author's progress toward subtler characterizations appears also in the way he summons up passing moods and intuitions. Thus we watch Simone groping for her own truth, vacillating between the active and the contemplative life. We feel her despair when she is betrayed, and we are moved by her sudden confrontation with Jacques's callousness and cowardice. Jaloux's sympathy for men and women whom an unjust fate has struck, and his ability to convey their hopelessness account for the heightened sensitivity of his introspective novels. As the author withdraws into the background, his characters become increasingly autonomous, and they reveal their deepest emotions through their own deeds and words: "Je ne vous en veux pas," says Simone to her rival, "j'ai trop souffert pour en vouloir à qui que ce soit. Si vous aviez souffert par amour, vous n'auriez pas été si mauvaise et si dure, mais vous n'avez souffert que d'amour-propre blessé . . . "[7]

Jaloux's aim to portray his characters in depth tended to refine his sensibility, and thus steered him toward the fragmented, the shifting and truly modern concept of characterization. The personages are no longer categorized immutably as good or evil; they are observed as they evolve in their relations with people at various stages of their life. At the beginning of the novel, for instance, the heroine inclines towards her brother's contemplative and esthetic life. Then, as she progressively becomes disenchanted with the barrenness of his purely abstract existence, she is seen coming more and more under the influence of her mundane sister. Finally, after sorrow has chastened her, she again draws closer to her esthete brother; this time, however, it is she who admonishes him to seek self-fulfillment by participating in life's experiences. Human relationships which, in Jaloux's first novels, were static and determined by the events of a fixed plot, now tend to bring out the inner growth of the characters. For the mutual influence which Simone and Robert exercise upon each other enables them to gain insight into their own self.[8]

When Robert, for instance, learns that his sister was deceived, he inveighs against her surrender to passion. Simone's answer to his carping reveals her mind and will. Against his arguments and sneers, she clings to the conviction that her own course of action was right, in spite of its disastrous consequences: "J'ai souffert, je souffrirai, c'est possible, c'est dans l'ordre. Mais j'ai été heureuse," she tells Robert. "Et toi, tu n'as jamais fait souffrir personne, mais à qui as-tu donné du bonheur? . . . "[9] In her sorrow, Simone feels at least that life has touched her, while her brother, who shuns the risks of personal involvement, proves to be, at that crucial moment, a dry and heartless theorist. The importance of human contact in creating a sense of change, is brought out most clearly in the effect which Simone's final tragedy has upon her brother. From the ironic and contemptuous young man that he was, he turns into a person filled with remorse and self-doubt.

Robert de Clausel's portrait indeed comes to life because it shows a person's transformation under the impact of unexpected happenings. On his first appearance, the young intellectual bears a striking resemblance to Sunhary, the caustic and detached observer of *L'Ecole des mariages*. His aloofness from his surroundings makes him the prisoner of ineradicable prejudices. In emergencies, when his real character comes to light, his ancestral instincts prevail over reason. Untouched by experience, Robert betrays the principles that he professes. For he has failed to integrate them into his personality. Nowhere else does Jaloux reveal the discrepancy between acquired attitudes and fundamental character more strikingly than in the portrait of Robert:

> La tolérance du plus large esprit n'entraîne pas fatalement semblable tolérance de sentiment. Ce que la pensée de Robert concevait, son coeur n'en savait rien. Ses idées pouvaient jouer à l'aise dans son crâne: elles n'enrichissaient pas son sang. Il coulait en lui, poussant dans ses globules la même force de routine et d'injustice, affluant avec de la colère et des sourdées d'envie et de rancune. C'était dans sa chair, dans ses fibres, dans son organisme qu'il avait mal; c'était là que, malgré tout, Simone était inexcusable, et ses sophismes philosophiques ne résistaient pas en face de son instinct.[10]

The author presents Robert gradually and from the distinct point of view of several persons. At first he is seen through the admiring eyes of Simone, standing far above the gay and frivolous society gatherings of her family, by his integrity, his love of art, his restless search after truth. Later, a friend of Robert brings out another side of the young man's character: his arrogance and pusillanimous fear of reality. ". . . vous flottez lâchement entre la métaphysique et la vie," he banters, "vous vous cantonnez dans l'art."[11] From the young man's elder sister, a final portrait emerges which emphasizes the egoist and the desiccated intellectual that she sees in him. Thus the novelist now brings out the many-sided facets of his personages, as well as their transformation in the course of time. The photographic realism of Jaloux's early period has been replaced by impressionistic sketches, which leave much to the reader's interpretation, and which bring out the multiplicity of characteristics coexisting within a single personality.

The portrait of Robert's friend, Marcel Déonat, seems at first sight by its fictitious and uniform characterization like a survival of Jaloux's earlier period of realism. At the beginning of the novel, that character does not come to life, for he is a mere replica of Gide's willful and restless heroes.[12] "Je brûle ma vie joyeusement, mais le temps n'existe pas, c'est l'intensité seule, qui importe," he exclaims, echoing the words of Michel, in L'Immoraliste. "Je veux être avant tout un vivant et non pas une ombre. Il faut repousser ce passé de routine, comme un papillon crève sa chrysalide, rejeter notre dépouille et jaillir vers le monde toujours neuf qui nous attend."[13] Déonat's conscious hedonism is too ostentatious to be genuine, too superficial to plead for life, or to stand as the antithesis of Robert's aloofness and somber misanthropy.

Nevertheless, Déonat is an arresting figure. On the one hand his craving for pleasure, his defiance of conventional morality, his baneful influence over others, give him a weird, Mephistophelean appearance that distinguishes him from the mean and earthbound characters of Jaloux's early novels. On the other hand Déonat's belief in the predictability of human behavior reveals the ingrained positivist. The interest of this portrait thus lies in its graphic illustration of the artist's conflict between the period's lingering determinism, and his own desire to cast off the moorings that bound him to a fixed tradition.

Poetic in tone, but with a commonplace subject, *Le Reste est silence,* another novel of Jaloux's transitional period, is related to *Le Démon de la vie* by its subtle characterization, and by the personal vision of reality which it conveys. The source of *Le Reste est silence* goes back to an incident of the author's youth. In the *parc Borély,* at Marseilles, where he used to play as a boy, Edmond one afternoon noticed a graceful woman, holding a child by the hand, talking to a handsome, but sullen young man. As the woman turned, the youngster caught a glimpse of her weary countenance. The recollection of that chance encounter provided him with the initial idea for the novel.[14] Another personal experience was instrumental in helping the author crystallize his plan for that novel. In his youth, Jaloux had read Jens Peter Jacobsen's *Niels Lyhne,* the story of a young man trapped in the contradiction between noble aspirations and the harsh realities of life.[15] The affinity of character between Mrs. Lyhne and her son Niels struck a responsive chord.[16] So completely did Jaloux identify his adolescent love for his mother with Niels's filial attachment that, years later, the emotional quality of that work and the wistful longing of its hero were to permeate the whole of *Le Reste est silence.*

The dreamlike atmosphere of this novel, which is set in Marseilles, as well as its descriptive technique, reflect the author's changing concept of reality. Jaloux entrusts the recounting of events to a narrator, Léon Meissirel, who attempts to resurrect in their original freshness the salient moments of his childhood. But the past is fleeting, and it refuses to surrender its secrets until an accidental sound, scent or visual impression miraculously revives it. Whenever these impressions occur, the narrator's stray recollections coalesce into an orderly pattern, and he thus experiences once more the emotions of his youth.[17]

Maurice Betz, a critic and novelist of the 1920's, noted a parallelism between Proust and Jaloux: "Dans les romans de Proust et de Jaloux, le passé et le présent se touchent et se pénètrent, leur oeuvre qui exhale le parfum d'un temps révolu, ressuscite le passé à travers un souvenir dont la réalité presque physique tout à coup nous émeut de nouveau."[18] The leading character of the novel is the innocent and distraught victim of a grave family conflict, and, as the narrator, is capable of communicating its dramatic quality, for he intuitively absorbed it as a child.

The boy's mother, a sensitive woman, had developed an aversion toward her commonplace husband, Joseph Meissirel, a middle-aged man who lived with clocklike regularity. Dissatisfied with her prosaic existence, Jeanne Meissirel envisions another kind of life, one that would come up to her romantic ideal of an intense and shared experience. She becomes intimate with a young man whom she met while taking her son to a playground in town. But the sullen young man whom she pursues and loves is loath to continue his relation with her, fearful of a lasting involvement. However Jeanne's repeated absences and her furtive manner arouse the suspicion of her husband. Joseph Meissirel interrogates his son, but the boy's replies are vague and ambiguous. A love letter that Joseph Meissirel intercepts confirms his suspicion. In the presence of his wife, he explodes in a frenzy of anger. The boy panics during that scene, as he is seized by a sudden fear that his mother will abandon him.

Léon's premonition of Jeanne Meissirel's departure proves to be accurate. Father and son are now anxiously awaiting her return. She comes back to her home only because her lover broke off with her. Resigned, but melancholy, she resumes her dull life with her husband.

The years go by. Léon is now alone and has grown into a reflective young man. One day he revisits the old haunts of his boyhood, and he is struck by a man who is staring at him. Léon suddenly recognizes the lover of his mother. By an almost irrational impulse, he is driven to shake the stranger's hand. For they share the recollection of Jeanne Meissirel, whose gentle and grieving expression their memory had kept alive.

Viewed primarily through the eyes of a child, that family drama serves as a means of emphasizing the paramount importance of subjective reality and intuition as guides to truth. As Armand Praviel notes in his discussion of this novel: "Jaloux maintenant se rend compte qu'il faut chercher la vérité, en soi-même et hors de soi, fuir les faux-semblants . . . et sous nos innombrables déguisements découvrir l'être intime, profond et vrai."[19] The characters' personal impressions and their nostalgic evocation of the past are superseding the visual descriptions of people and their surroundings which characterized Jaloux's early work. The narrator lets his imagination wander:

> . . . Maintenant ce passé renaît sous mes yeux, à mesure que j'écris. Bien des détails m'en reviennent. C'est comme un pastel très fin, qui s'animerait lentement, et remuerait un peu. Une poussière irisée se soulève autour de moi. Comme cela est triste et charmant! Les pires heures de ce temps lointain seraient exquises à revivre. . . . Nous ignorions l'avenir, et nous nous désolions. Mais l'air chaud et comme imbibé de fleurs de ce soir où maman était partie, — comme je le respirerais volontiers encore! Oui. . . . Et j'ouvre ma fenêtre pour chercher dans l'atmosphère de la nuit ce quelque chose de spécial que j'aspirais ce jour-là.[20]

As he recalls the past, Léon Meissirel experiences it again so intensely that his words communicate to the reader the sadness of a motherless child; thus he recaptures the life of the events he summons up.

Evocative fragrances, images and music now replace the active memory in reviving the atmosphere of bygone years. Past and present intermingle whenever the sound of an old tune brings back to Léon's mind his childhood days, his home, his young mother playing the piano at nightfall:

> ... quand j'entends aujourd'hui (les sonates de Beethoven ou les nocturnes de Chopin), il me semble que leurs harmonies sortent du fond même de mon coeur. Je ferme à demi les yeux, j'oublie le salon où je suis, l'être qui promène ses doigts sur le clavier; je revois ma mère avec ses cheveux bruns, ... avec ses grands yeux bleus, . . . son profil droit, ses mains soyeuses et douces sur ivoire marbré de noir. Voici l'ancien fauteuil où je m'asseyais, ... voici les coussins de vieille soie, devenus presque humains à force d'usure et de soumission ...[21]

This intuitive perception reflects Jaloux's own evolution from an external and photographic realism to the expression of an intimate and heartfelt reality. Indeed, the quest for authenticity accounts for the growing role that the author assigns to the child as the beholder of an invisible, but essential truth.[22]

Like the prescient narrator in *Du Côté de chez Swann*, like the youngsters in *Le Grand Meaulnes*, who are filled with dire forebodings of evil, Léon Meissirel has the child's premonition of an impending calamity. "Du fond de mon ignorance," he recalls, "quelle soudaine sagesse me venait, quelle intuitive expérience?"[23]

At the same time, Jaloux's characterization of his personages has become more attuned to the spirit of the century. After the manner of Proust and Alain-Fournier, he suggests the elements of mystery in human character, and like them he tries to reach the person in depth. He achieves this new dimension by summoning up the nocturnal scenes of his characters' sleep. For example, he describes the nightmares that assail the boy on the eve of his mother's escape. These dreams express a child's consternation at his helplessness, his bewilderment in his loneliness. It is by delving into the deeper recesses of consciousness that Jaloux has attempted to reconstruct the boy's dreadful feeling of utter misery.

The child's receptiveness to every mood, sensation and impression will enable him later to remember the fading past. It is, in fact, this capacity to relive crucial episodes of his childhood that breathes life into his vignettes of the provincial bourgeoisie and into his sketches of Marseilles.[24] For in the evocation of his early youth, Léon dwells on familiar places, so as to convey their inherent poetry and charm. He describes, for instance, the *parc Borély* where he accompanied his mother on her secret rendezvous. In his attempt to revive the atmosphere that permeated the places of his youth, the narrator resorts to colorful images and similes:

> Nous descendîmes au seuil d'une double allée, au bout de laquelle s'ouvrait le parc Borély. Un petit château de couleur jaunâtre semblait s'adosser aux collines, et, de sa terrasse à la grille d'entrée, des bassins se suivaient, jetés dans le gazon comme des pièces d'argent. Les ombrages un peu courts des arbres laissaient glisser le soleil, comme un filet aux mailles trop larges échapper des poissons. Quelques rares voitures roulaient doucement sur le sable fin.[25]

Comparing the factual descriptions of the early *romans de moeurs* with this subtle evocation of Borély Park, the change in style is remarkable. The cold enumeration of objects has been replaced by a romantic personification which endows nature and things with feelings. Thus the castle in the park, like some shepherd in the mountains, seems to rest against the hills, and the sun rays on the foliage shimmer like goldfish in a pond.

There is hardly any trace left at this time of the concrete realist in Edmond Jaloux. The deserted streets of Marseilles are seen through the nightmares of a frightened child: "La rue monte; les becs de gaz, en allongeant leurs reflets dans la boue, y tracent de petits chemins dorés. . . ."[26] Similarly, the old harbor of Marseilles looms in the fog like a gigantic ghost. "Tout avait un air abandonné, solitaire et triste," the narrator remembered, "comme si le commerce qui se faisait là ne se fut entrepris qu'avec des morts ou avec des ombres."[27] His descriptions of Marseilles' somnolent neighborhoods also reflect the narrator's mournful outlook as he recalled the dreary winter Sundays of his youth. "Le dimanche pesait lourdement sur la ville, et les magasins fermés donnaient un air lugubre aux longues rues."[28]

Deserted and forbidding, these outlying districts reflected the isolation of Marseilles' middle class families, their fear of being intruded on, and their withdrawal behind the protective walls of their old dwellings. Jaloux's description of the city provides a sharp insight into the mentality of the French and southern bourgeoisie, into people made restless by time which lies heavy on their hands.[29] The feeling of a slow moving, almost static time is conveyed in this novel by the stagnant environment, by the monotony of Sundays, by the force of provincial routine. The narrator recalls these seemingly endless days: "Le dimanche, nous nous promenions toujours ensemble. C'était la même flânerie sous les arbres, et, avant de rentrer, l'ennuyeuse visite à ma tante Trémelat."[30] Sometimes the child would walk with his preoccupied and absentminded father: "Nous suivions le chemin coutumier de nos promenades hebdomadaires, machinalement, comme les chevaux d'omnibus, au retour, continuent leur route vers la remise, sans y être dirigés par le cocher."[31] These humorous touches about bourgeois life possess an intense reality, and they reflect the inner growth of the novelist as a man and as an artist.

Convinced that intuitive knowledge was a more faithful guide to an understanding of reality than visual perception, Edmond Jaloux now proceeded to reveal the truth hidden beneath M. Meissirel's mediocre and uneventful life. For in this humdrum existence there was a human tragedy. Meissirel feels insecure because of the inequality of condition between himself and his wife. She craves adventure and the refinements that riches afford; while he finds happiness in the domestic pleasure of a family outing. This discrepancy of tastes and interests serves only to intensify Meissirel's consciousness of his own mediocrity. That feeling, though not fully rationalized, nevertheless grips him with persistent force. His confusion and anxiety appear in the reiterated questions he asks his son about the young woman's frequent absences; he shows his sense of powerlessness and dependence upon the child, during Jeanne Meissirel's brief flight from home. Léon evokes the mood of the unhappy man:

Il s'était moins assis qu'effondré sur un fauteuil, et il respirait difficilement. Et j'eus soudain une grande pitié de cet homme. Rentrait-il, le front chargé de menaces ou tout prêt à oublier ces choses mystérieuses dont il avait accusé ma mère? Je vis bien à son attitude que jamais il n'aurait imaginé sa maison vide. Je distinguai, en un clin d'oeil, son désarroi, son incertitude, son angoisse.[32]

These rhythmical and flowing sentences communicate the boy's intuitive grasp of his father's anguish and dismay; the simplicity of the language bringing out the insidious power of unformulated but deep-seated fears.

The importance which Edmond Jaloux attaches to feeling and intuition in *Le Reste est silence* confirms his growing interest in the domain of the irrational. That new emphasis endows his characters with a mysteriousness that was lacking in his earlier *romans de moeurs*. Unlike the personages of *Les Sangsues* and *L'Ecole des mariages*, who were either saints or sinners, the principal characters of his recent novels are neither altogether heroes nor villains. They appear as complex individuals whose nature brings into play the whole spectrum of human emotions, and are therefore more convincing than the black-and-white sketches of Jaloux's initial phase.

The novelist shows his deepening grasp of man's ambivalence and instability by revealing his characters in the throes of a personal crisis. After Jeanne has left her husband, following their violent quarrel, the unfortunate man, as we saw, is crushed by grief. Intuition has enabled Jaloux to penetrate beneath the façade of conventional appearances and superficial impressions, which in his early novels distorted his vision, and presently gave him an intense awareness of the complex and changing human personality.

Edmond Jaloux, therefore, sensed in *Le Reste est silence* that the character differences between husband and wife doomed the marriage of a devoted and unselfish man. For Jeanne Meissirel, filled with yearning for a great love, which her mediocre husband cannot satisfy, is a romantic and subtle character. In creating that personage, the author drew from a variety of sources. In appearance, Jeanne Meissirel resembles the woman whom Jaloux had observed at Marseilles in the *parc Borély*. Her inner self, however, is a composite of a great many women whom the author had known, and doubtless contains also reminiscences of his mother.[33] While observation still constitutes the groundwork of Jaloux's portrayal of character, his aims have changed: "Le vrai rôle du roman est de mettre en action le drame intérieur que chacun de nous vit dans l'ombre."[34]

In reality, as Daniel Mornet has pointed out, Jaloux's protagonist in this novel is another Madame Bovary.[35] Like Flaubert's heroine, Jeanne's education in a convent school, and her love for the dramatic aspects of the liturgy, have given her a poetic bent as well as a taste for luxury. Living in her dream world, and ill prepared for the realities of life, Jeanne is dissatisfied, like Emma Bovary, with the cycle of mediocrity, routine and boredom in which she is caught. To find the love that would provide an escape from her everyday life, Mme Meissirel is prepared to abandon even her family. She is driven, therefore, to lead a life of fraud and deception.

But it is not Jaloux's intention to moralize. Rather, the author strove to present the situation from the point of view of the characters themselves, and thus has moved away from his former adherence to objective realism. Above all, he wants to enlist the reader's understanding of the tragedy of human loneliness. The narrator thinks of his mother's desolation, and of his own anxiety which he inherited from her:

. . . j'avais entrevu cette chose effroyable qu'est l'isolement de chaque être et son caractère incommunicable. Mais je ne saisissais pas alors, comme je l'ai deviné depuis, que cette torture de la solitude morale, où nous nous débattons à mort, je ne l'éprouvais que parce que ma mère en avait souffert plus que moi et avait tout fait — hélas! — pour échapper à son angoisse.[36]

Again the simplicity of the language sets off the fervor of unexpressed emotions. This gift of translating into words the silent but tempestuous feelings of the personages distinguishes, in fact, the warmly personal style of *Le Reste est silence* from the ironic tone of Jaloux's early period of realism.

If his first novels were essentially satiric, it is because he viewed his personages with the detachment of an impassive observer. In *Le Démon de la vie* and *Le Reste est silence*, Jaloux's ability to experience the trials of his characters accounts for their inwardness. Anxious and isolated beings are groping for a happiness that seems forever to elude them. By their nostalgic quest for an ideal life that would ennoble their existence, the characters of Edmond Jaloux's novels of individual experience are warmly appealing.

The substance and characterization of *Le Reste est silence* neatly balances elements of realism and of introspection.[37] The provincial wife who longs, in her ennui, for the closeness of a deep friendship, is a familiar story that links *Le Reste est silence* to the regional novel of the nineteenth century. Jaloux, however, has renewed the theme of conjugal

71

strife and infidelity by presenting this drama through the sensitive vision of the child who witnessed it. Moreover, the characters' way of expressing their inmost feelings, illustrates the growing importance of subjective reality, as well as the author's own emancipation from his initial and photographic realism. In this way Jaloux's submission to the concrete object gradually waned as it imperceptibly gave way to a personal and poetical view of the world.

Part III
THE POET

CHAPTER V

THE NOVELS OF POETIC IMAGINATION

In his early novels, Edmond Jaloux sought to represent man concretely, in a specific time and milieu, as if he were being described by an impartial observer. By 1906, however, the novelist became dissatisfied with this purely factual vision of life. In order to convey a more subtle image of the human personality, he turned to such other methods of perception as intuition, feeling and personal experience. The usual device that he then employed was to reveal the characters from the point of view of different people, or to show reality through the sensitive vision of a child. But in spite of these attempts to refine the art of characterization, the psychology of *Le Démon de la vie* and *Le Reste est silence* does not differ essentially from Jaloux's period of naturalism. Side by side with revelations of the inner man, we continue to get detailed descriptions of hereditary traits and external appearance, as well as a faithful rendition of dialogue.

That period of transition was followed by another literary phase which extended from 1913 to 1920 and revealed a more genuine aspect of the author's temperament. We saw that Edmond Jaloux read symbolist poetry with enthusiasm in his youth; that he himself started out as a minor symbolist poet.[1] His feeling for the musical quality of language, which he tried to suppress during his early naturalist phase, now rose again to the surface and transformed his method of writing. While his works of this period are essentially studies of psychological analysis, their prevailing mood differs markedly from the problem novels that can be found among

75

writers of an earlier generation such as Bourget and Boylesve.

These last-named authors emphasized, like the naturalists, the inevitable influence of environment and education on the development of character. Jaloux, however, was moving away from the sociological approach to the study of man. For he now sought to retrace the sinuous movements of thought and emotions that constituted his characters' inner life. In the introduction that he wrote to *Cinquantenaire du Symbolisme,* a description of an exhibit held at the *Bibliothèque Nationale* in 1936, Jaloux explained the transformation that the French novel underwent between 1905 and 1920 from a naturalistic approach to an inward and personal mode of characterization:

> Il ne s'agissait plus de savoir comment s'exprimaient les blanchisseuses, ni de connaître les usages du petit bourgeois, ni quelle importance avait pour l'avenir d'un individu, les tares que lui légaient ses parents, mais de donner force et chant à ses émotions, à ses images, à ces analogies . . . à ces apparitions de la conscience souterraine, à ces rencontres des événements intérieurs, à ces rêves enfin, qui font à notre vie son tissu le plus véritable. . . . Toutes les conséquences du Symbolisme n'ont pas encore été tirées.[2]

This interest in man's inner life explains the prevalent concern with memories of childhood. For the nostalgic quest of a lost youth is a major theme of early twentieth century writers such as Proust, Alain-Fournier, Giraudoux and Jaloux. The concept of personality, which their works reveal as an ever changing process in the course of time, is similar to the Bergsonian idea of duration or fluid consciousness. Like the philosopher of "creative evolution," these novelists dwell on the cumulative and unique development of the individual's affective life.[3]

But their growing awareness of the elusive and personal character of human feelings brought out the shortcomings of classical prose as a means of expressing these sentiments. It is not surprising, therefore, that the novelists of this period were captivated by the flowing movement of symbolist poetry. Combining words into rhythmic and sinuous sentences, that cast a spell on the reader, they succeeded in recreating the original impressions of fleeting moods or of intimate experiences. By means of subtle analogies and metaphors, they discovered behind the confusion of external phenomena, the harmony of an essential and ideal world. Moreover they felt, as had the symbolists before them, the inherent unity of the senses, and they tried therefore to resurrect the totality of the past through the poetical device of synesthesia.[4]

The first of Jaloux's novels in which the shift from naturalism to poetic imagination becomes clearly apparent is *Fumées dans la campagne,* which he wrote on the eve of the First World War. Significantly the book opens with the return of the narrator to his native town where the quaint sites, evocative names and subtle odors orchestrate in symphonic fashion and revive for him the whole of his vanished youth:

> Ayant tourné à gauche, je suivis la rue de l'Opéra, rue étroite, malgré son nom emphatique, rue sévère, montueuse. Une porte ouverte sur une cour laissait voir un hôtel magnifique, dont les hauts pilastres corinthiens fleurissaient la façade. C'était l'hôtel de l'Estang-Parade. . . . J'aurais voulu une fois encore visiter ses pièces discrètes, respirer leur odeur d'encens et de vieilles boiseries, qui, mieux que mon infidèle mémoire, m'eût rendu l'aspect de Calixte.[5]

The plot of this novel, however, is rather conventional. Raymond de Bruys, the scion of a distinguished family of which several generations had resided at Aix, was left an orphan on the death of his father, when he was but eleven. A few years later, his mother was remarried to Maurice de Cordouan, a landscape painter who had yet to prove his worth. In his late teens, Raymond enrolled at the local University, and there met Calixte Aigrefeuille, an independent girl who attended the University, and who organized a *cénacle* in her home. Raymond introduces his stepfather to Calixte who promptly falls in love with the handsome Cordouan. Faced with that unexpected turn of events, Raymond, who loves the girl himself, experiences deep pangs of jealousy. His mother, an earnest and reserved woman, is shaken by her husband's faithlessness, and soon thereafter, is stricken by paralysis. Her would-be artist husband dissipates his energy in a number of other affairs, ending up as a bohemian, leaving his promise and his aims unfulfilled. *Fumées dans la campagne* thus illustrates the decline of an established provincial family, and also the vanishing of youth's hopes and illusions.

But if the plot tends toward the commonplace, the novel itself occupies an essential position in the evolution of Edmond Jaloux as a writer. An important change has taken place in the descriptive technique. At the beginning of his career, Jaloux tended to picture the environment with the exactness of a photograph. In the novels of poetic imagination, however, the portrayal of the locale is entirely subjective, as though transformed through the prism of the narrator's feelings. Raymond de Bruys is moved by the sites of his childhood: "Lorsque, au sortir de la gare, je vis, à l'entrée du cours Mirabeau, la grande fontaine, bruissant entre ses femmes et ses lions, mon coeur battit, et je crus que j'avais cessé d'être un solitaire, un éternel étranger."[6]

Thus, *Fumées dans la campagne* is noteworthy above all as a poetic evocation of the city of Aix and as a touching recollection of a man's youth. As the narrator saunters on the *cours Mirabeau,* the town's main thoroughfare, with its rows of elms, its staid eighteenth century mansions, its fountains and statues, he becomes detached from everyday concerns, and is drawn into meditating about enduring values. The harmonious spectacle that unfolds before his eyes heightens the interplay between his emotions and the stillness of the surroundings:

Je défilais devant les platanes, devant les magasins démodés, devant les vieux hôtels: hôtel d'Espagnet, hôtel de Nibles, hôtel d'Arbaud-Jouques. Ces vocables retentissaient à mon oreille comme des noms historiques! Et puis, ces pilastres inscrits dans les façades, ces balcons aux ferronneries légères, ces portes sculptées de moulures... dont la couleur épaisse faisait valoir l'éclat d'un marteau de cuivre, ces cariatides à la musculature contractée! Que voilà donc une cité selon mon goût! Une grandeur que rien ne nécessite plus, beaucoup de majesté autour de beaucoup de solitude, et un grand silence afin de mieux entendre les voix du passé![7]

The author's method of suggesting atmosphere clearly illustrates the stylistic changes that have taken place since his early period of realism. In Jaloux's regional novels of manners, words were used impersonally to convey an objective meaning; in the novels of poetic imagination, they are chosen for their euphony or for the mental associations which they induce. Such expressions as "magasins démodés," "vieux hôtels," "noms historiques" all speak of a bygone age. These words thus suggest the nostalgic mood of the novel.[8]

Other innovations appear also in the narrator's description of the Provençal countryside. Living scenes that bring out the various physiognomies of nature under a constantly changing sky now substitute the bleak and frozen pictures of the *romans de moeurs:*

Avec des cris aigus, les hirondelles déchiraient l'air d'un vol rapide, comme un coup de faux; une paix dorée flottait sur le jardin. De légers lilas tendaient leurs quenouilles violettes si fraîches que leur parfum se mêlait à celui de l'herbe mouillée. Les nuances vertes des feuilles semblaient neuves du matin. Des boules-de-neige, comme de grosses houppes, poudraient des buissons, le soir retentissait du coassement d'innombrables grenouilles, et une étoile qui venait de pointer semblait une déchirure dans l'azur, comme si tout le ciel allait se déchirer de même et montrer derrière sa doublure bleuâtre, un lumineux univers couleur d'argent![9]

In retrieving the atmosphere of the setting, Raymond de Bruys relies almost exclusively on sounds, colors and fragrance. As was true of the narrator in *A la Recherche du temps perdu,* the blending of these sensory impressions renews his contact with the past by linking his childhood with his revived memories.[10]

And yet, the narrator's rediscovery of that past has poignantly reminded him of the ephemeral character of all human experience. In the autumnal landscape of Aix, where he watches the burning of dead leaves, and the rising smoke melting away, he sees an image of our brief and insubstantial destinies: "... l'odeur des feuilles se mêlait à l'air: odeur âcre, vivifiante et agréable, odeur de bois vert qui flambe. J'y trouvais un plaisir mystérieux et bien connu, fait du souvenir des automnes anciennes où, enfant, on a déjà l'intuition que les vacances sont courtes, les heures heureuses, vite finies, toutes les affections menacées, et où l'on écoute... les leçons de l'incertitude humaine!"[11] His intuitive knowledge and poetical vision make him look beyond concrete appearances, to the general and symbolic meaning of a site.

Edmond Jaloux's portrayal of character in *Fumées dans la campagne* likewise reflects a new way of contemplating reality. We here find a subtle awareness of man's complexity, a fact that marks a significant departure from Jaloux's early portrayal of the human personality as made up of a cluster of immutable traits. Similarly the author now strives to convey the feeling of a person's evolution over a long period of time. Unlike the hero of *Le Reste est silence*, who continued to observe and report events as a child, the protagonist of *Fumées dans la campagne* develops gradually from boyhood into maturity. Thus we feel the child's jealousy during the period of his mother's courtship, the adolescent's confusion when he is spurned by the girl he loves, the man's nostalgia as he revisits the places of his youth.

The symbolist movement had attempted to reintroduce into literature the spirit of mystery as well as the feeling for intimate moods and for the authentic imagery of the self. Introspection and the need to express the complexities of inner life thus became the major preoccupation of the novelists who were in any way influenced by that school.[12] The personages are often beset with doubt, leaving the reader to form his own understanding of their nature. In Jaloux's novels of manners, the characters were generally cast in a simple mold. Barbaroux, we saw, was the incarnation of saintliness, while Augulanty represented only fraud and treachery. On the other hand, the novels of poetic imagination present individuals torn between opposing feelings. The narrator remembers his feverish youth and the conflicting personalities that struggled within his breast:

De tant de frères jumeaux qui se défiaient et combattaient pour obtenir la prééminence, un seul est demeuré! C'est lui qui me conseille ces pages, et nous regardons ensemble au fond du miroir que nous tend notre mémoire, ces êtres ardents, romanesques, généreux, combatifs, qui du temps de ma merveilleuse adolescence, se bousculaient l'un l'autre et luttaient à qui irait le plus loin, qui partaient ensemble pour la vie et dont il n'est resté aujourd'hui que le plus misérable et le plus chétif![13]

While Jaloux's early *romans de moeurs* demonstrated the

inescapable effect of environment on character, his novels of the individual attempted to show how personalities react under crises. Only in the novels of poetic imagination does the author's intuition allow him to penetrate into the mind of his characters. We are thereby enabled to grasp the narrator's train of thought, and to follow the process by which an ebullient youth becomes a disabused man. We then realize that, in the process of aging, he has won an insight into himself which the fixed personages of *Les Sangsues* were never able to attain.

Jaloux's portrayal of Cordouan similarly reveals the intuitive and poetical approach of the author's middle years; for the picture is a subtle one, suggesting the bright and shadowy aspects of the personality as well as the irony of fate. When we first encounter Cordouan, he strikes us as the typical Provençal, jovial and irrepressible, but also boastful and vain. At the outset he seems extremely engaging; as time goes by however the first impression proves to be quite misleading. The exuberant and outgoing manner conceal a vacillating character who is incapable of confronting the rigors of artistic creation and who flees invariably into a world of fantasy, where he no longer needs to overcome obstacles and disappointments. "—J'ai des projects sans nombre," he exclaims, "la vie est trop courte! Jamais je n'aurai le temps de les réaliser! Je porte en moi tant d'oeuvres qui ne demandent qu'à voir le jour!"[14]

Cordouan imagines himself as a great artist, who will some day achieve renown. But instead of cultivating his talent, he spends day after day confiding to others all his thoughts and projects, beguiling his listeners with his innate charm and eloquence. "Il parle sa vie," noted the critic Paul Souday, "et croit avoir agi lorsqu'il n'a que bavardé."[15] His naive enthusiasm is a harbinger of his wretched fate. When the promise of youth fails to materialize, the fog of illusion that Cordouan needed in order to live gradually evaporates leaving the aging painter face to face with himself, defeated and humiliated.

Since they were viewed from the outside and represented only a single dominant trait, the characters of Jaloux's realistic novels generally failed to arouse any sympathy. Cordouan, we saw, is a composite character, drawn with lucid penetration, but also with that community of feeling which shows beneath the man's reckless ways, the pathos and the endearing qualities of a truly poetic temperament. "Une source véritable de poésie était dans le coeur de cet homme . . ." remembered the narrator, "quand il versait sur nous ses illusions, on en était tout englué."[16] His selfishness and irresponsibility, though they form an intrinsic part of his personality, are largely unconscious aspects of it. If he first undermines and finally destroys the happiness of his family, he is at the same time destroying himself. He thus becomes an almost tragic hero, who, for all his very real faults, evokes nonetheless a feeling of genuine sympathy.

In the portrait that Jaloux draws of Lucie de Bruys, the narrator's mother, the author reveals his new technique of suggesting the elusiveness of personality, by sketching her in many light strokes, thus achieving an impressionistic effect. For the heroine does not stand revealed at once, as she would have been in the author's naturalistic novels. Her idiosyncrasies come to light gradually as the story unfolds. At the beginning of the drama, Raymond is unable to fathom the melancholy mood of his mother. The narrator like the reader have yet to realize that a morbid strain runs through her family. Lucie's father had taken his own life and after that tragedy, her mother had spent in deep mourning all of the years that remained to her. The revelation of these facts, however, comes only in the denouement of *Fumées dans la campagne.*

Intuition plays a major part in the gradual unraveling of the character of Lucie. Fragments of conversation that Raymond overhears gradually reveal to him his mother's real nature. During his naturalistic period, Jaloux had developed his personages by disclosing only concrete details about them. Thus we find out about the fall of Elodie Guitton, the

83

principal character in *L'Ecole des mariages,* through a minute description of her impoverished surroundings.[17] In *Fumées dans la campagne,* we are given as guidelines only random, but highly significant traits. For example, Lucie's bitter quarrel with Cordouan saddens her son; it also puzzles the boy, for his knowledge is not clear having come through bits and snatches. "La conversation se termina là," he explains, "du moins devant moi."[18] In a similar vein, the enigmatic destruction of a beautiful chrysanthemum gives Raymond a glimpse of his mother's jealous fears. Once more insight mingles with uncertainty to provide a subtler vision of reality. ". . . ma mère ne savait rien de précis, mais qui soupçonnait elle? Je l'ignore. Sa sensibilité trop fine la mettait en garde, mais contre quoi?"[19] The portrait comes alive as opposite traits of Lucie's personality are described side by side. Her austerity is the product of an innate sense of duty, and of her need to believe that man can be a noble, almost perfect creature. Jaloux does not, however, hold her forth as a paragon of womanhood. The narrator who reads signs of despair in his mother's growing religious ardor, expresses his own fears and apprehensions:

> Je redoutais qu'à la longue, elle devînt aussi inhumaine qu'elle était déjà sévère et qu'elle perdît cette hauteur de vue, cette indulgence que j'avais accoutumé de trouver en elle et qui . . . cédait la place à un esprit quinteux, à cette tournure pharisienne, que donne trop souvent l'abus des fréquentations religieuses et cette vanité d'être des élus, que l'on ressent, quand on se groupe entre gens de même paroisse, autour du même curé, quand on en arrive à considérer les autres comme de pitoyables damnés.[20]

Lucie's puritanical cast of mind is the cause of much unhappiness. She develops before our eyes until she assumes her full stature. For Jaloux now seeks to communicate the changes that occur in the person over a long span of time.

At the end of her life, when repeated betrayals and humiliations have weakened her powers of resistance, and when physical paralysis strikes, she becomes a tragic figure.[21] Her faith in human nature has been supplanted by hopelessness, fear and the anticipation of death: "Elle se traînait en s'appuyant sur une canne, lentement, péniblement, comme un oiseau dont les ailes sont brisées."[22] By means of poetical similes that evoke images of injury and death, the author communicates an intense feeling of the ravages wrought by life on a woman imbued with a high sense of duty. Moreover, in order to suggest the complexity of her character, Jaloux has forsaken the concrete and factual method of his early period, and has adopted instead the intuitive techniques, as well as the metaphorical language of symbolism. Thus, when hope momentarily dispels Lucie's fears and suspicions, the fragility of peace is brought home, not by direct statement, but by a subtle analogy between the changing expression of the woman's face and the uncertainty of an April day:

. . . dans une seconde, je vis la figure de ma mère se transformer, comme le ciel se transforme, quand le vent emporte les derniers nuages et qu'à la glaçante giboulée succède le soleil, et tout aussitôt, elle s'assombrit de nouveau.[23]

When he remembers Calixte, the narrator is particularly nostalgic, and in drawing her picture, he betrays the idealization and the enthusiasm of the youthful lover. As the reader observes the girl through the fond recollection of Raymond, the portrait he beholds has the poetical quality that is typical of a sentimental evocation of the past. Calixte recalls to the narrator the world of his youth. Aix, with its old regime façades, which in Raymond's fertile imagination conjured up scenes of *émigrés* of the Revolution fleeing on a dark night. The young man remembered Calixte as a vivacious and caustic girl, who was the life of any party. He also summons up the memory of her by recreating the light, color and ambience of the time when he used to court her, thus reviving old emotions and resurrecting the earlier experience in its totality. The narrator remembers Calixte and the setting with which she is indissolubly linked:

> Un rayon de soleil, glissant par la haute fenêtre, luisait sur le carrelage couleur de miel, dont les dalles étaient inégales à force d'usure. Le ciel dur et cru avait l'éclat de l'émail, et tout y semblait incrusté. Les feuilles commençaient de poindre aux rameaux du figuier. Je regardais la poulie rouillée du vieux puisard pendre à sa potence verte. Ces humbles aspects composaient à mes yeux un paysage unique. Quand je songeais à Calixte, le soir, chez moi, devant ces photographies de fresques que je ne parvenais pas à comprendre, je voyais derrière son image ce grand carré d'azur inaltérable, et ce figuier aux branches qui serpentaient, et ce puits, et la couleur aussi de ces carreaux cirés et jaunes. Et cet ensemble que je croyais perdu, je le retrouvais avec joie comme un groupe d'amis que l'on croyait à l'étranger et que l'on revoit soudain dans une maison pleine d'indifférents![24]

Though she was witty and gay in her youth, Calixte like the other characters of this novel, becomes a different person in the course of time. While the narrator resided in Paris, she married a local teacher and removed herself from the social whirl of the town. She now adopts the way of life and the prejudices of a dutiful middle class wife. Only when Raymond sees her again, when he reminds her of his old affection, of the time of their youth, does she admit that her earlier gaiety, her independence of spirit and her ironic contempt for bourgeois values have all but disappeared. In this portrait Jaloux again brings out the gradual transformation of attitude that takes place in the course of a lifetime. While he showed Cécile turning suddenly into a shrew, in *Les Sangsues*,[25] the author emphasizes, in his novels of poetic imagination, the slowness with which people change, as he illustrates the inevitable loss of enthusiasm and the gradual waning of spontaneity.

At first sight, the character of Miette, the housemaid, recalls Flaubert's selfless and devoted servants, such as Félicité, in *Un coeur simple*, or Catherine Leroux, the farmhouse drudge in *Madame Bovary*. However, the narrator envisions Miette under the magic screen of poetic imagination. Instead of providing a concrete description of her physical appearance and surroundings, as he would have done in his early novels, the author offers a suggestive portrait of Miette by relating the plain, yet sensible folk wisdom that is hers, and the kindness which she radiates. Jaloux thus enlarges the portrait of Miette until she comes to personify the stoic virtues of patience, devotion and work. After a lifetime of service, even after the death of her employers, she remains in the homestead, keeping a silent watch over the family hearth. Raymond, now a man of mature years, thinks of her: "Je compris quelle féerie délicate il y avait dans l'âme obscure de Miette."[26] As he departs from his native Provence, he eulogizes the old servant:

J'emportais la vision de Miette, assise au coin de son foyer désert, comme une fée domestique appliquée à son travail modeste et veillant sur mes morts, belle dans son humilité, comme quelque image ineffaçable et presque effacée du souvenir.[27]

Drawn with feeling and nostalgia, such characters endow a novel like *Fumées dans la campagne* with the true accent of poetry. But if the subjective vision enabled Jaloux to acquire a more penetrating insight into human nature, it did not safeguard him from a tendency to idealize his people or to view them through the halo of faded memories. While their provincial existence recalls the naturalistic tone of an earlier period, the propensity to ennoble their actions and to emphasize the universal meaning of their life, lifts them into the higher realm of poetry.

This bent for thinking in terms of general truths and analogies influenced Jaloux's outlook until the early 1920's. He again resorted to a blending of sounds and colors for the setting of his new novel, *La Fin d'un beau jour*, which he wrote between 1919 and 1920. Likewise, Jaloux went on to show his characters through the technique of synesthesia, a method which fostered direct confrontation with one's past and most authentic self. Even after the First World War, he continued to feel the magic of the symbolist *rêve*. But an experience that the author underwent during the war was instrumental in broadening his horizon. We saw that he served in a military hospital, and this gave him an immediate contact with the realities of war.[28] Jaloux now turned inward, and his deepened awareness of life was reflected in a new conception of the novel of poetic imagination that was shorn of all superfluous literary and decorative elements.

Jaloux's discovery of the novels of Henry James in the early postwar years also played a part in modifying the tone and subject of his later novel of poetic imagination as he sought to penetrate more profoundly into the mysterious workings of the mind, and as he attempted to convey the darkening atmosphere of a landscape at sunset.[29] The influence on *La Fin d'un beau jour* of James's *Death of the Lion* is quite obvious.[30] That short story relates the sudden rise to fame of an elderly writer, and the abuse to which he is subjected by a coterie of acquaintances. One young woman, however, greatly admires his artistry, and ends by falling in love with the aging novelist. But if Jaloux borrowed elements of James's plot for his own novel, his adoption of the Jamesian technique is more significant. For in both works, events are told from the point of view of an outsider whose limited vision compels him, as if he were a reader of the story, to discover the personages, and to make out the meaning of their doings. The gradual transformation of the narrator's blurred vision into a fairly distinct image, simulates

88

life itself, with its shadowy and enigmatic appearances that slowly clear away.

La Fin d'un beau jour appears primarily as a study of character. Joachim Prémery is a famous author who proclaims a philosophy of detachment from the concerns of everyday life. He believes that nature's laws are binding on all mankind, and, like the Hindu philosophy expounded in the Bhagavad-Gita, he advocates the necessity of acquiescing in one's fate, regardless of its harshness. For only through such an acceptance, Prémery maintains, can a man secure peace of mind, which he regards as the highest good. But that stoical attitude towards life does not fill the writer with a sense of contentment. He is cold and aloof, and scarcely maintains a close relationship with anyone. As he was visiting his colleague Hallencourt, a student of Byzantine history, he meets the scholar's daughter, Olive and falls in love with her despite the great discrepancy in age. Now his reserve and icy indifference give way to liveliness and warmth of feeling. Olive idolizes the novelist; Prémery, however, arrives at the realization that their age difference constitutes an unbridgeable gap to their union. The writer finds a pretext for loosening their relationship in the attention that a younger man pays to Olive. After a while, Olive responds to the latter's advances. With the passage of time, Prémery experiences a great void in his life, for the remembrance of his relationship to Olive arouses in him intense sorrow and self-doubt. He is aware, however, that he can no longer change the course of his life, and he returns to the solitary existence of the artist.

Versailles is the locale of this novel, and Jaloux's description of that town introduces new aspects of phantasy and hitherto unused imagery. Flowers appear, as in a dream like wax stars; the gardens of Versailles are seen through the glaucous light of an aquarium: "... une nuit verte flottait sous les arbres, traversée de stries d'or."[31] At times the eeriness of Jaloux's descriptions would indicate a shift of focus from the external world of matter to the fleeting imagery of inner consciousness.

However at other times, the blending of sense impressions brings back the immediacy of the whole scene:

> Nous remontions vers le Grand-Trianon, dont les colonnes roses palpitaient dans la rose couleur du soir. Une odeur poussiéreuse de lilas semblait prise dans le papillotement lumineux de l'air.[32]

The novelist's description of sunset in Versailles recalls the nostalgic poetry of Albert Samain. Both writers excel in suggesting the sadness of a passing day, both experience anew the thrill of memorable moments through the stimulus of color and of scent.[33] "Soir d'or" is an expression that recurs under the poet's pen to convey a twilight scene; "rose couleur du soir" or "roses d'or" are the novelist's favorite images in rendering the mystery of nocturnal moods.

This work, as we saw, is distinguished by a dreamlike imagery that was missing in the earlier poetic novels of Edmond Jaloux. The main palace of Versailles, surrounded by a wreath of clouds, for example, seemed from afar like the legendary castle of the Fair Mélusine. As the narrator tramples through the fallen leaves in the gardens of Versailles, he visualizes the multicolored tapestries of the later Middle Ages. Odd formations of clouds remind him of the silhouette of one of the Mages' faces, of chariot races, and of the variegated plumage of the peacock. When the sun has set, and its reflection on the window panes has disappeared, the narrator fancies that some ghost has drawn a black curtain over them:

> Une à une, les fenêtres du palais s'éteignaient; le foyer de roses d'or, pris dans toute vitre, se plombait avec effroi; on eût dit qu'un fantôme invisible tirait derrière chaque croisée un rideau de fer. Les pierres elles-mêmes s'assombrissaient, transmuaient leur matière poreuse et saline dans cette matière sans nom dont les ténèbres sont faites.[34]

The transformation of the landscape under the fading twilight is a theme that links Jaloux to the decadent poets of sunset and evening.[35] For he shares with them a sense of life's mystery before darkness. His sketch of Versailles, therefore, is not a concrete and finite picture, but the soul and the essence of nature at nightfall.

The description of the personages in *La Fin d'un beau jour*, also reveals the author's grasp of hidden, but fundamental truths, as he strives to convey his characters' fleeting moods, their imperceptible changes of sentiment, and the sadness that grips them at the irretrievable flight of time.[36] Jaloux's attempt to illuminate the life of the mind and the evolution of thought, sets apart the novels of poetic imagination from his earlier works. For in the latter works the characteristic traits and ideas of their youth tended to remain unchanged throughout their lifetime. Jaloux's new method of characterization implies the subtle analysis of passing states of mind and feelings in order to give the impression of the mobility of the individual.

The author's increasing reliance on intuition and on the new viewpoints, which Bergson's psychology and the poetic revolution of the 1880's had developed, enabled him to go beyond the static concept of personality and to trace the evolution of Joachim Prémery's life. We see his transformation from an aloof intellectual, who devotes himself to discovering the principles of human behavior, into a person who himself is subjected to the full range of emotions:

> Il avait alors senti de nouveau qu'une force subtile et douce pénétrait en lui et que sous son influence, il éprouvait des émotions oubliées, des émotions qui le rapprochaient de cette humanité, qu'il ne jugeait depuis longtemps que comme un répertoire d'équations psychologiques.[37]

Thanks to his inward vision, Jaloux is now able to communicate the wanderings of the mind beyond the confines of rational thought, and also the battle that rages within the hero, as he seeks a path between his traditional set of principles and the unexpected surge of feelings by which he is being carried away: "Il marchait à pas redevenus prudents, comme celui qui n'est plus sûr de sa route. A la joie de tantôt succédait l'angoisse, une angoisse si lourde que le monde n'était plus devant lui qu'un catafalque énorme, enfermant le cadavre d'un dieu."[38] In *La Fin d'un beau jour*, Jaloux is striving, therefore, to capture complex and subterranean currents of thought. Every day of the hero's life brings forth new attitudes. Jaloux not only delves into the inner recesses of Joachim Prémery's consciousness, he also allows his hero to be seen through the eyes of several witnesses. By this many-sided approach, the author is able to bring out the complex and unforeseeable nature of man, and thus shows once again that he has broken with the deterministic vision of his early years.

Like the "jeunes filles en fleurs" who were admired by young Marcel at Balbec, Olive Hallencourt, Prémery's beloved, appears as a fragrant, evanescent creature, refracted in the prism of poetic imagination. For he saw her as an ideal person — the incarnation of youth, beauty, and transparent spirituality. " . . . je voyais l'insaisissable Olive glisser sur ces parterres d'or, comme une fumée radieuse, à peine plus dense que les parfums de septembre."[39] Again the blending of sense impressions and the use of poetic similes evoke an idealized vision of a loved one. Like Calixte in *Fumées dans la campagne*, Olive is a romantic personage. So thoroughly has she immersed herself in Prémery's work, that she reenacts in her own life the world of fiction of the man she reveres. Yet the impression we retain of her is at once lifelike and subtle. For the narrator illuminates her nature in a veiled and guarded way, and never fully elucidates the mystery that surrounds her. As the critic Henri Bidou aptly remarked:

Le roman nous donne des personnages principaux la

connaissance que la vie nous en donnerait. Et cette connaissance est souvent bornée par l'ignorance par des doutes, par l'impossibilité de comprendre.[40]

Fumées dans la campagne and *La Fin d'un beau jour,* two novels that Jaloux wrote between 1913 and 1920, therefore mark a significant departure from the author's initial adherence to a deterministic and visual concept of reality. These works also differ from Jaloux's later novels of the individual in that they envisage man, not as the victim of unexpected misfortunes, but as the unwitting accumulator of the experiences of a lifetime. For the novelist now seeks to bring out the authentic person, who lurks behind the accident of habit and social convention. While the characters of his regional *romans de moeurs* were tied inexorably to a specific time, class and place, the personages of the novels of poetic imagination have, by their inner growth and development, acquired attributes of universality.

In order to project this enlarged vision of existence, Jaloux had felt the need of renewing earlier themes and techniques. By establishing a subtle correspondence between sensory impressions, as the symbolists had done, he was able to revive his characters' memories of childhood, and thus to illuminate the whole range of their inner life. Moreover, the transformation of the writing, from a purely factual to a rhythmic and metaphorical style, allowed the novelist to express the most tenuous shades of feelings as well as complex and obscure processes of thought. Thus Jaloux's return to the poetical spirit of his own youth, enabled him to give form to his personal vision of the world, and to make astonishing progress in his exploration of the hidden self.

Chapter VI

THE NOVELS OF PSYCHOLOGICAL EXPERIMENTATION

The beginning of the 1920's marked the advent of a new stage in the literary evolution of Edmond Jaloux. Although his work of that period continues to emphasize the characters' inner life, it differs markedly from the novels of poetic imagination. We saw that *Fumées dans la campagne* and *La Fin d'un beau jour* portray idealized people enshrined in a dreamlike setting, as they are reflected through the nostalgic recollection of a narrator.

The First World War, which undermined the framework of European society, simultaneously witnessed a revolutionary transformation in the content of western culture. Among the many innovations that rejuvenated European civilization, psychoanalysis was one of the most significant. This new method of analysis took hold in France in the immediate aftermath of World War I. The first translations into French of the work of Sigmund Freud, which appeared in 1921, stimulated a keen interest in the principles and concepts of psychoanalysis.[1] Its success in supplanting the old mechanistic notion of the unified personality with the dynamic vision of man, as the battleground of contradictory selves, was destined to exert a profound influence on the literature of the 1920's.

André Breton was one of the earliest French writers to use Freudian techniques in exploring the vast stretches of the mind that extend beyond the domain of rationality. Like the Austrian neurologist who interpreted the spontaneous utterances of his patients, Breton recorded the verbal flow of his own subconscious and thus created an entirely new style. Known as automatic writing, this mode of expression was used jointly by Breton and Philippe Soupault in *Les Champs Magnétiques,* a work whose unusual and vivid language evoked the fantastic scenery of dreams.

But if Breton drew inspiration from the techniques of psychoanalysis to recapture the enigmatic language of the subconscious, other writers such as André Gide and the playwright H.-R. Lenormand adapted the new methods to broaden the scope of their characterization. Thus the daydreams of Boris, the nervous child in *Les Faux Monnayeurs,* and the minute analysis of Lenormand's troubled heroines bring to light the hidden conflicts of the authentic self. Similarly, novels such as *La Bonifas* (1925) by Jacques de Lacretelle and Jules Romains' *Lucienne* (1927) lay bare, through unending analysis, the desires and inner struggles of the characters. By means of the interior monologue, these authors enabled the reader to penetrate inside another mind and to fathom its mystery.

Edmond Jaloux's experience during the war as an anesthetist in a military hospital had given him a deep interest in the problems of psychology.[2] In early 1924, writing for *Le Disque vert,* a literary and scientific journal, he expressed his belief in the validity of the new science:

> . . . pour quiconque a réfléchi sur la nature humaine, il est incontestable qu'il est impossible aujourd'hui de se passer de quelques-unes des idées du Dr. Freud: le refoulement, la censure, l'ambivalence, le symbolisme mental, sont aujourd'hui des théories qui apportent une lumière évidente dans des problèmes qui demeuraient obscurs.[3]

These psychological preoccupations appear in *Les Profondeurs de la mer* and *Soleils disparus,* two novels of the twenties which illustrate the subtle relation between consciousness and the subconscious.[4]

95

In 1922 Edmond Jaloux published *Les Profondeurs de la mer*. Unlike the novels of poetic imagination which summoned up the events of a fading past, this story is told by the characters in the fervor and the confusion of their actual experiences. But the directness of the narrative, accounts for its feverish tone and incoherence. In this novel therefore the reader needs to rearrange for himself the haphazard images, sensations and ideas that cross the characters' minds. On the perceptiveness of the audience and on its ability to share the emotions of the characters depends the illusion of reality.

The plot of *Les Profondeurs de la mer* may be reconstructed as follows. Claude Lothaire, a middle-aged playwright residing in Paris, has enjoyed a very successful career. He grows tired, however, of writing facile comedies to which he owes his great popular vogue. Lothaire craves a solid literary reputation, and he therefore turns to serious drama which, he hopes, will confer it. But his first attempt in that direction ends in total failure. Despairing to retrieve his shattered fortune in Paris, and loathing the Philistinism of the general public, he decides to withdraw to Abbazia, a port on the Adriatic Sea. There he meets an English couple, David and Gwendolyn Grove, and though accompanied by his wife, falls in love with Gwendolyn. Their liaison is cut short, however, by the Groves' sudden departure from Abbazia. The two have scarcely left the harbor than their ship runs into a storm and sinks. David and Gwendolyn perish in that disaster. After he receives the distressing news, Lothaire sets out to reclaim the bodies, in order to bring them back to England.

The shock of the fate that befell the Groves prompts the playwright to question his system of values and the meaning of his own existence. In his search for a valid aim in life, he revisits the places where he had spent his youth, and begins to realize the fatuousness of his dreams of glory. He rejoins his wife in Abbazia, a wiser man, for he has now forsaken fame, having resolved to devote his remaining

96

years to writing plays that expound his philosophy, without regard to the dictates of popular acclaim.

Distinct changes in Jaloux's approach to the structure of his plots emerge in the course of his development as a novelist. In general, these changes are indicative of his gradual assimilation of the characteristic introspection of the twentieth century. As the novelist perfected his technique, he gave increasingly an inside view of his characters, the expression of their fleeting thoughts now forming the substance of a loose, almost anti-plot.[5] In Jaloux's naturalistic novels, it will be recalled, the action was rigidly structured and predetermined. In the novels of poetic imagination, however, Jaloux broke entirely with his early determinism. The function of the plot was then reduced to bringing out the development of the characters over the span of a lifetime. But it was only in Jaloux's psychological novels of the 1920's that the traditional plot disappeared altogether, and that the action acquired reality only after its many disparate strands had been woven together by a knowledgeable reader. This shift from a circumstantial to a purely subjective plot explains why Jaloux now unfolds the story as it is relived by the hero himself.[6]

In his treatment of time, Jaloux likewise departs from the path that he has trodden hitherto. We saw that the *romans de moeurs* which he wrote at the beginning of his career were situated at a definitive stage of time. In the two subsequent phases of his evolution as a writer — in his novels of the individual and in those of poetical imagination — Jaloux likewise chooses a definite moment in time as the temporal setting for his works. In his early novels, the unfolding of the story faithfully mirrors the chronological order. In his novels of the 1920's on the other hand, time sequences are blurred, external events appearing at random as the personages actually perceive them. Thus, the principal events of Claude Lothaire's life cross his mind in a haphazard way. "Mes jours passés," he recalls, "se pressaient confusément à ma mémoire, déformés par le ton général des pensées

97

que je venais d'exprimer, n'assemblant dans leur lamentable réunion que ce qu'ils avaient eu de triste et d'avorté."[7]

Jaloux was drawn by the contemporary trend toward inwardness and he attempted, therefore, to capture the essentially subjective character of time. In setting down the personages' train of thought, he endeavored to show that past, present and future are inextricably merged in their consciousness. For instance, Lothaire accelerates and condenses time as he glides mentally from one event of his life to another:[7a]

> Un moment de faiblesse, et moi aussi, je coule à pic! Quelle misère! J'ai besoin de toute mon énergie, si je veux garder le sentiment d'une vie active et féconde, d'une vie *vivante*, comme je disais autrefois dans mes années d'enthousiasme, si je veux obtenir Gwendolyn qui me fuit, si je veux me prouver encore que mes ennemis n'ont pas raison de me proscrire. . . .[8]

We learn about the failures of Claude Lothaire through allusions to his actual predicament. Similarly the reader becomes aware of Lothaire's earlier success by comparing his present chagrin with the remembrance of his fruitful past.

The story of Les Profondeurs de la mer thus takes form as the audience coordinates for itself the thoughts, dreams and stray impulses of the characters. In Jaloux's novels of poetic imagination, it will be recalled, the personages were revealed gradually as they evolved from youth to middle age. That method was a legacy from the realism of the nineteenth century. Claude Lothaire's first person narrative, on the other hand, brings out simultaneously every aspect of the hero's mental life, in its contradictory and haphazard manifestations. We get a glimpse of the intricate workings of the protagonist's mind, we experience his anguish, and we perceive the somberness of his mental imagery. In a soliloquy, Claude Lothaire unwittingly reveals some of his obsessive thoughts:

Les images les plus opposées se mêlent en moi:
Gwendolyn et Tolosano réunis, la houle des spectateurs,
le soir de la répétition générale de *Prométhée*: une
marée de visages narquois, indignés, blasphémant de
colère ou de mépris, les regards haineux, les bouches
tendues pour siffler.[9]

Haunted by visions of hostile crowds which rekindle the
playwright's jealousy and anger, he suffers diffusely without
being able to read into his own mind. For the images follow
each other without sequence as in a dream, expressing the
tumult below the level of worded thought.

In his novels of poetic imagination, we saw, Jaloux tried
to convey the moods and passing emotions of his characters.
But a narrator who was almost invariably present, imposed
an orderly development upon the complexity of man's existence. From the early 1920's onward, however, Jaloux sought
to probe more deeply into the feelings and the consciousness
of his personages. That attempt prompted him to turn to
such a new method as the inner monologue. In *Les Profondeurs de la mer*, for instance, the hero communicates directly his state of mind, his mood, his perplexities:

J'entre partout comme un condamné, comme un
assassin. Je gêne et j'interdis chacun. On se tait devant
moi, on n'ose pas me regarder en face quand je parle
de certains sujets. Trouverai-je donc partout ce fantôme
qui me harcèle et qui me contraint de penser à lui? Il
y a des moments où je me dis qu'il vaudrait mieux
mourir que de se survivre ainsi.[10]

From first to last the protagonist analyzes his sense of
defeat and the void that now surrounds his life. Jaloux
presents his hero grappling with his own contradictions, and
in search of his lost identity.[11] Lothaire's minute description
of his emotions gives us an insight into the subterranean
regions of his conscience. But this excessive inwardness — an

inwardness which excludes action altogether — leads to a fragmentation of reality. Some twenty years after the publication of *Les Profondeurs de la mer,* Jaloux declared that this atomization of the personality actually corresponded to our modern view of man:

Chaque être est constitué par des myriades d'émotions, de rêves, de projets, d'intuitions, de pressentiments, de souvenirs, . . . tous fragmentaires, tous inachevés, qui nous bombardent de leurs chocs minuscules, comme les atomes de la science moderne.[12]

This pulverization of reality mirrors the revolt which erupted in the aftermath of the First World War against the accepted rationalist assumptions about man. The hero of Jaloux's novels of the 1920's strives to discover himself in the confusions and inconsistencies of his inner life. This quest is not, therefore, a rational undertaking. It is a constant interweaving of many experiences and intuitions that continue to recur in memory and to disappear and that no more respect regular time sequence than they do in actual life. Thus Claude Lothaire reacts to the death of Gwendolyn not in a sudden outburst of sorrow, but in a long and wistful recollection that he nurtures by summoning up her presence through accidental sense perceptions. Claude Lothaire was musing:

Les mêmes passages d'ombres, de lumières, les éclairages identiques de la saison, des odeurs oubliées qui renaissaient curieusement avec telle date du calendrier, me rendaient par moment et plus fidèlement que ma mémoire sans force, des impressions si vives de la présence de Gwendolyn, que les mille souvenirs physiques et moraux qui y étaient attachés renaissaient soudain en foule, m'assaillaient d'un foisonnement de réalités inexistantes. Alors brusquement, dans un éclair, à tra-

100

vers une multitude de résurrections sensorielles, Gwendolyn reprenait vie....[13]

Here the Proustian device for recall of Jaloux's earlier period merges with his new technique of presenting inner time.

As Claude Lothaire is growing old, he gradually overcomes his thirst for fame, his envy and passion. "Cet être avide, turbulent, passionné, épris de toute chose, toujours impatient, toujours à l'état de désir, l'avais-je été vraiment?" [14] he wonders. During his younger years, the act of striving and succeeding had always constituted in his eyes the quintessence of life. He was essentially an unprincipled climber and an egoist. But in the time of his maturity he came to realize the vanity of his thirst for fame. Having given up his dreams of glory and become reconciled to a life of obscurity, he was able for the first time to appreciate nature's beauty: "Je me plaisais à donner une telle attention à ce que je voyais," Lothaire remembered, "que j'avais l'illusion de le devenir un moment: nuages qui couraient au ciel, avec leur hâte de l'extrême automne . . . feuille qui tombait comme une pièce d'or démonétisée . . . étang qui miroitait, pie qui sautait de branche en branche." [15] His belated pantheism fills him with a pervasive serenity. By a strange quirk of fate, it is his discovery of nature that makes Claude Lothaire conscious of his final regeneration. He has at last come to realize that he can know himself only as he understands the relationship that binds all living things.

The hero's counterpart, the earnest and unspoiled Gwendolyn, appears to the reader mainly through the eyes of Claude Lothaire. He sees all kinds of feelings reflected in her limpid eyes. But the development of her personality, as in his case, does not proceed along the beaten path of sequential narration. It is only through the character's occasional remarks, through the stray recollections of her lover that her portrait emerges, and then only in a fragmentary manner. Individual traits, which seem ambiguous at first, become clear only later as in reality where people are revealed to us slowly and in a sporadic way.[16]

By projecting the main incidents of this novel through the eyes of the protagonist, Jaloux gives the reader the sensation of participating in his mental life. But the hero's continued self-analysis leads to a disintegration of his personality. Claude is giving his thought a free rein:

L'hiver fut glacial et maussade sur cette côte devenue entièrement solitaire. Je m'enfonçais dans mon spleen et ma misanthropie . . . J'avais comme un besoin d'aller jusqu'au fond de ma détresse, de l'épuiser, mais elle se renouvelait sans cesse.[17]

The thoroughness of the main character's self-examination and the consequent dispersion of reality convinced Jaloux that he had exhausted the possibilities of the psychological novel. In order to arrest this tendency toward disintegration, Jaloux began to experiment with new techniques. He now sought to draw together all of these disparate elements into a synthesis, by fusing dreamlike visions with conscious reality. In creating a magic world of fiction, Jaloux followed new trends in the literature and in the pictorial arts of the 1920's as manifested in the poetical plays of Lenormand and in the allegoric, phantasy-ridden canvases of James Ensor.[18]

Soleils disparus, a novel that Jaloux completed in 1927, was one of the first in which that new vision is fully apparent. A man's attempt to escape from a stifling environment and recapture a lost Eden constitutes the main theme of this work. Raymond Valtier, a teacher of Greek and a person of delicate feelings, obtains a position as a tutor to Queen Erica of Illyria. A gifted and cultivated woman, Erica resides in her castle of Adelsgratz, a sumptuous mansion set in an oak forest. Valtier has scarcely assumed his new post than he establishes a profound kinship with Erica. He shares with her an affinity for the arts and a general sympathy of views and convictions.

But these halcyon days are cut short by Erica's violent death. Deeply shaken by her disappearance, Valtier has no choice but to return to France, and resume his old humdrum existence. The meanness of his latter-day life, which is intensified by his recollection of his recent stay at the Illyrian court, drives him into despair and finally into illness. He soon improves, however, his recovery being due in a large measure to the solicitude of Valentine Guerrée, a musician who resides at the same boardinghouse as he. Valtier subsequently marries, though another girl than Valentine, but he continues to be haunted by the recollection of Queen Erica. For his wife's frivolity and her fecklessness serve only to underline the magnitude of his loss. Though Valtier eventually divorces his wife, their separation fails to restore his equanimity. The remembrance of Erica and of his all-too brief acquaintance with her, continues to obsess him. That preoccupation ends by driving him slowly into insanity. Valtier's madness proves to be incurable. Valentine, who had not ceased to love the wayward teacher, arranges for his confinement in a hospital for the mentally ill. Imagining in his clouded brain that he had returned to the castle of Adelsgratz, the unfortunate Valtier has regained at last his inner peace.

Jaloux's choice of the theme of insanity in *Soleils disparus* constitutes a break with his traditional subject of an artist's life. For on the eve of writing this novel, he was discovering with enthusiasm Gérard de Nerval and the imaginative German writers of the early nineteenth century.[19] It is particularly in the aforementioned French novelist's work, *Aurélia*, in which extraordinary dreams acquire the force of reality in a man's quest for a woman, as well as in such fantastic tales by Ludwig Tieck as "Der blonde Eckbert", in which the author communicates his characters' irrational terrors, that Jaloux drew inspiration for his own novel of psychological imagination.[20]

A number of critics maintain that *Soleils disparus* is essentially a novel of escape. For instance, André Billy and Franz

Hellens emphasize the characters' propensity to seek refuge in dreams.[21] Likewise, Louis-Jean Finot and André Germain regard the imaginary adventures of the hero as his only defense against the meanness of his surroundings.[22] An element of escapism is doubtless present in this novel. Jaloux loathed the new order that emerged from the First World War, and that witnessed the breakdown of the genteel tradition in which he was raised. He deplored the mindless rush for profit, the growing mechanization of life and the concomitant passing of individualism, as well as the increasing perfunctoriness of social relationships. Strong feelings about his own time, therefore, incited him to shun what he regarded as its harsh realities.[23]

However, in *Soleils disparus,* the yearning to transcend the boundaries of immediate reality supersedes mere escapism. For the hero of this novel exemplifies the conflict between the spiritual quest of the individual and the social surroundings that oppress him. Raymond Valtier seeks to free himself from the restricted environment of his boardinghouse and to enter a liberated world of dream and imagination. The charmed life that Valtier is leading at Adelsgratz keeps him in a state of euphoria. Sometimes he imagines that he is journeying through many different countries to seek a perfect woman, one who embodies all of the qualities of Queen Erica. At other times, he fancies that he is transplanted into the Athens of the Golden Age and partakes in its philosophical disputations. The ambience of the royal court and his recurrent fantasies are more real to Valtier than the town life which he occasionally observes as he ventures beyond the threshold of the castle. When Valtier had entered upon that fabled interlude of his life at Adelsgratz, "... il lui semblait avoir franchi un seuil d'oú l'on ne revient pas vers ces choses."[24]

We here observe the coalescing of the dream and of the waking state to the point where fancied and actual experiences have become indistinguishably merged.[25] Valtier's sojourn at the castle of Adlesgratz assumes in his eyes a reality that later surpasses his own penurious existence as a teacher of Greek. For his poetic experience at the side of Erica realized a deeply felt longing for a life of beauty and led him to delve into his inmost self. One by one he shed the blinders that had separated him for such a long time from his true self. "... il lui semblait que les bande-lettes qui avaient jusque-là enserré son âme se défaisaient l'une après l'autre; il découvrait en lui, dans sa propre ima-gination, un trésor jusqu'ici insoupçonné."[26] Imagination now supplants introspection and the internal monologue, for the author no longer seeks to discover the hidden con-flicts of the self. He draws inspiration from the world of vision and fantasy to bring out an integral representation of man. For instance, in *Soleils disparus*, the characters reveal their own selves, not through brooding self-analysis, but rather by the summoning up of their yearnings and their dreams. Jaloux expresses the new aim of the novelist: "... l'auteur cherche moins à observer le monde extérieur que l'autre, c'est-á-dire un univers plus poétique et psychi-que que psychologique, un univers qui soit celui des ima-ges et des allégories inconscientes et non des sentiments et des passions."[27]

In creating the character of Erica Von Oertling, Jaloux shows likewise that he has forsaken the psychological approach for a more imaginative vision of man and of the world. Instead of seeking to capture the elusive reality of the changeable self — as he had done in his novels of in-trospection — Jaloux now attempts to link, in a coherent representation, the multiple facets of the human persona-lity. It is, therefore, Erica's personal view of things that reveals her true nature. For example, she sees in the glisten-ing necklace which she throws into the lake of Lauriena, a reflection of all the repressed feelings, hopes and impulses that are embedded in the human consciousness. "Ah! si on pouvait descendre au fond des consciences, c'est encore lá qu'on trouverait le plus de perles jetées!" she confesses to Valtier. "Que de trésors gaspillés, que d'affections perdues sans retour, que d'aspirations mutilées!" [28] Moreover, Erica views the fountains that rise in the lake as symbols of man's persistent inclination to reach for inaccessible goals.[29]

By uniting dreamlike visions to reality, Jaloux offers a portrayal of his personages that differs markedly from the fragmented image that we encountered in the psychological novels of the early 1920's. That new characterization differs also from the novels of poetic imagination, such as *Fumées dans la campagne* and *La Fin d'un beau jour,* in so far as the latter were devoid of uncontrolled dreaming and fantasy. Jaloux now achieves that integral reconstruction of his personages through the creation of a universe that is based almost exclusively on his seething imagination.

The novelist appeals also to the imagination of the reader when he evokes the scenery of *Soleils disparus.* For a series of weird images flash across its pages, and they form a dreamlike, yet strikingly vivid world. Jaloux's exhaustive description of the castle and of its surroundings in no way resembles the photographic copy of a familiar site. He depicts Erica's residence by transforming shapes and textures in order to bring out their unusual aspects. Built entirely of coral, the façade of the palace has curved lines which imitate the undulation of the waves or of spiral shells. The garden and the castle appear through a succession of concrete images: "C'était une suite de terrasses, scandées par de grands escaliers blancs; en haut, un petit palais rococo, rose et jaune, tordait ses volutes de coquillage terrestre. . . ."[30] The interior of the castle appeals also to the audience by its strangeness and originality. Gigantic tapestries, representing stylized kings and queens struggling to seize one another's realms, adorn the huge walls of the main hall. Like the palace of king Minos on Crete, the castle of Adelsgratz is a labyrinthine network of deserted rooms and winding staircases, in which Valtier would have lost his way but for the presence of an occasional usher, dressed in a gold and crimson livery.

The park that surrounds the mansion abounds in deer, antelopes and other denizens of the forest. Mythological statues and fountains spraying multicolored waters crowd its approaches. "L'atmosphère était si lourde que Valtier avait l'impression de déplacer en marchant des nuages." [31] In the wood there is a lake that is covered with water lilies. That wood is studded, moreover, with pagodas, constructed entirely of porcelain. When the wind blows through the forest, rustling its leaves, it whines as though it uttered a lamentation. This scenery is bathed in mist, for the sun never penetrates through the thick foliage of the park of Adelsgratz, and distances shrink as happens invariably in dreams:

> Un brouillard étrangement doux montait avec le soir, dissolvait les contours de chacune des choses qu'il caressait, mais, par contre, comme un arpenteur consciencieux, il restituait aux différents plans leur vraie distance. De la plus haute terrasse de Lauriena, qui domine toute une vallée, la Reine et Valtier voyaient ainsi chaque ligne de terrain se détacher des autres, . . . pour former un mince mur de fumée, d'où émergeaient les mille peupliers, clochetons d'une ville d'Ys noyée dans ses feuilles. La molle rivière, qui déroulait au fond du paysage son cours sinueux, était de lait et d'or; un encens pâle effaçait ses rives, et les collines, que l'on aurait dû apercevoir derrière elle, s'étaient évaporées, bues par le soleil couchant. [32]

To the queen and Valtier, who from a turret in the castle were observing the valley in which the river flowed, the village of Adelsgratz seemed like a city in a German folktale:

> Les faubourgs d'Adelsgratz apparurent, avec leurs bicoques peintes, leurs grands toits, leurs balcons extérieurs; puis les rues des vieux quartiers, bousculant

leurs maisons à échauguettes, leurs pignons, leurs jardins tapis derrière des portes à sculptures baroques, leurs boutiques reculées sous des auvents.[33]

When Valtier leaves the enchanted domain and returns to Paris, the resumption of his drab existence profoundly saddens him. He had always considered himself isolated from other men and marked for an exceptional destiny. The recollection of his memorable days at Adelsgratz serves only to aggravate his woe.[34] His dreamlike remembrance of this glorious interlude in his life assumes more and more the force of reality. He becomes so dependent on his imagination that on his wanderings through Paris, he sees the city exclusively as in a fantasy: "Les arbres des quais font le gros dos sous l'averse. La Seine se hérisse de fléchettes. . . . Dans la nuit qui m'étreint, je fais danser ces billes aux mille couleurs qui enflamment mon esprit."[35] The capital then appears to him shrouded in weird hues, particularly sea green, as if it had been transmuted into an aquarium. This fantastic vision of his psyche gradually superimposes itself on the outer world and the novelist, omniscient no longer, merely steps in to voice the character's inarticulate anguish:

> Le bruit de Paris arrivait maintenant par vagues stridentes. Raymond . . . avait peur de rentrer dans cette foule avec laquelle il n'avait aucun intérêt commun. Le ciel s'assombrissait de nouveau. Saurait-il retrouver seul le chemin du royaume où sa mère et la Reine l'avaient presser d'entrer?[36]

Significantly Jaloux ends on a note of doubt. But the perceptive reader intuits that Valtier's mind is slowly giving way.

In his two principal novels of the 1920's — in *Les Profondeurs de la mer* and in *Soleils disparus* — Jaloux strives to extend his concept of man and to take possession of his inner reality. He attains these goals by making use of such devices as the inner monologue and the portrayal of dreams. The author is no longer concerned with recapturing the past, as was the case in his novels of poetic imagination. Rather, he seeks to express the present moment in all of its chaotic manifestations. The general trend toward inwardness which these novels exemplify is not the only element of modernity that they contain. For the reader is now required to reconstitute in a meaningful pattern the many disparate elements of a fragmented experience. He achieves that result by viewing the world through the imagination and the point of view of the central character.

In *Soleils disparus*, Jaloux creates an artistic vision that unites the realms of illusion and reality; the frontier that normally separates these realms having vanished. But in so doing, he does not altogether renounce his deep-rooted attachment to reason. Among the many literary doctrines that vied for his allegiance — ranging from the stream-of-consciousness technique to surrealism — Jaloux ultimately chose a position midway between conscious thought and fantasy.

Part IV

THE SEEKER OF AN INVISIBLE WORLD

CHAPTER VII

THE NOVELS OF MYTH AND SYMBOL

Until the late 1920's the evolution of Edmond Jaloux as
a novelist had corresponded to the dominant literary trends
of his time. In the last phase of his development, however,
Jaloux became estranged from the prevailing currents of
French thought. The early 1930's witnessed the rise of a
literature of social protest, the most outspoken representatives of which were Louis-Ferdinand Céline and André
Malraux. The former author's *Voyage au bout de la nuit*
contains a fierce denunciation of contemporary civilization.
That novel points up some of the crucial problems of our
time: man's enslavement to the machine, the uniformity
of modern life, the alienation of the self in a world bereft
of hope and meaning. Like Céline, the author of *La Condition humaine* revolted against the absurdity of the human
condition. Malraux, however, eschewed the temptation of
nihilism by plunging into revolution and by finding in that
struggle a justification for man's existence.

But Jaloux could not follow the path chosen by these
rebels. Though a traditionalist in his politics, he also
sensed the crisis of the West as well as the decline of the
individual, dwarfed by the bigness of modern technology.
Jaloux's belief that he was living in a period of disintegration, and his concern for man's position in the cosmos,
prompted him to have recourse to ageless symbols and
myths.[1] In the ancient civilizations, myths illustrated the
numerous enigmas of human existence with great clarity
and forcefulness.[2] Jaloux's own interest in the perennial conflict between fatalism and free will, explains also his belated tendency to envision the world through myths and

113

symbols. By establishing a parallel between his own creatures and their Greek prototypes, he was able to bring out
the universal relevance of an individual life. For the personages now exemplify a certain attitude towards existence
and thus become types of human destiny. Also symbolic
of universal issues and dilemmas are the characters' prophetic and oracular dreams.

If Jaloux sought to transcend the limits of time and space
through the intermediary of myths, he also introduced them
in the novels of this period for artistic reasons. The association of a specific myth with a given character poeticized
the life of ordinary mortals; the mythical way of thinking
thus helped to unify the fragmented impressions of experience into a parable.[3] Moreover the visions recurring in
the characters' dreams denoted the existence of another
world, rich in poetic and universal meanings. *La Grenade
mordue* and *L'Egarée*, which constitute the principal works
of Jaloux's period of myth and symbol, bring out a pattern
of images that symbolizes, as we will see, some important
aspects of the human condition. The key images of these
novels: the Seine river, a haunted castle in Provence, a
forest, all express in a concrete manner the invisible power
of fate. Symbolic associations thus become a medium for
communicating the mysterious forces of life. Ultimately
Jaloux's quest for transcendence would manifest itself in
a type of fiction uniting the unseen and the visible world.

This fusion of reality and imagination appears in *La
Grenade mordue* which Jaloux wrote in 1933. For that
novel recreates the story of Persephone, who in Hades ate
the pomegranate, the bitter aftertaste of which vitiates the
flavor of all earthly nourishment. Persephone's fateful act
forced her descent into the realm of the dead. But in spite
of the legendary element that the plot contains, its structure
has a familiar pattern. Patrick Séléré is a master of por-
traiture. His originality as an artist wins him a circle of
close friends who meet regularly in his studio to discuss
questions of painting and of life. Claire Berger, the young

and earnest daughter of a deceased friend, belongs to this group and seeks guidance from its debates. François Englebert, a struggling art critic who also attends the meetings, becomes enamored of Claire.

One day, an art dealer, Charles Malgouyres, visits Séléré's atelier in order to discuss the sale of some of the artist's work. Claire happens to be present at the time of his visit, and immediately feels drawn by his extraordinary self-assurance. Her infatuation is so great that she quickly agrees to marry the assertive young man. But their union is not a happy one. Malgouyres's involvement with other women makes Claire intensely jealous; his infidelity, far from lessening the force of her passion, serves only to reinforce it. Séléré, who maintained his friendship with Claire throughout the time of her marriage, observes her despondency and becomes apprehensive of a catastrophe. With François Englebert, he decides to visit the disconsolate young woman. Having entered her apartment unannounced, the two men find her as she is about to take her own life, and save her from death.

A separation between Claire and her husband ensues, and soon thereafter they obtain a divorce. Gradually, thanks to the warm concern of her two friends, Claire recovers at least the appearance of her former self. Englebert, whose love for the young woman has remained undiminished from the time when he first met her, renews his advances and offers to marry her. But she declines his proposal, for her attempted suicide has drained her of all emotion and given her an intimation of death that she is incapable of casting off. It is the sudden and brutal collapse of her illusions that have robbed her of all enthusiasm for life and left her as a mere shadow of her former self.

In this novel, as we shall see, myth and symbol give archetypal significance to the chaotic reality of the individual. The narrator of *La Grenade mordue* is the aspiring art critic François Englebert. In order to show the man behind the façade of social conventions, Jaloux still uses the

115

technique of the inner monologue, particularly to evoke certain moments of crisis. For example, when the narrator fears that some misfortune will befall Claire Berger, we perceive all of the images that cross his mind:

> Claire m'apparaissait comme au jour de notre première rencontre, à peine plus réelle qu'une des femmes peintes, debout sur les chevalets. Elle marchait dans le parc de Saint-Cloud, faisant craquer sous ses chaussures la dernière neige de l'hiver. Elle fondait littéralement devant le regard de Charles Malgouyres....[4]

Moreover, when Englebert finds the young woman in a state of total collapse in her attempted suicide, he suddenly envisions himself participating in a sacrificial offering, of the kind that the ancient Greeks performed. "Comme dans un sacrifice antique," he recalls, "je croyais ne faire qu'un avec la victime."[5]

If there are elements in Jaloux's phase of myth and symbol that hark back to an earlier time, this creative period reveals nevertheless a number of original traits. Now he no longer attempts primarily to delve into the psyche of his personages; he seeks rather to crystallize their states of mind into their corresponding poetic components. Claire, for instance, is not only the object of François' affection; by her presence she also helps him to evoke the places that they had visited together, and the ambience that permeated these happy moments. In a larger sense, Claire incarnated for Englebert all that has beauty and meaning:

> Je regardais derrière Claire la grande nuit pure qui s'élevait, toute chargée de ses cristaux suspendus, et plus bas, à notre niveau, la longue mer de Paris, avec ses éclairs, ses colonnes de lumière, ses longs tracés d'or, ses espaces sans couleur, ses moutonnements immobiles, ses îlots obscurs. Tout cela aussi, je l'embrassais à travers Claire. Elle n'était pas seulement un être unique, perdu

dans la multitude des êtres, mais quelqu'un qui partici-
pait de la manière la plus intime et la plus violente à
tout ce qu'il y avait autour de moi de beau, d'éphémère
et de fulgurant.[6]

Similarly, when Englebert's hopes of marrying the girl he
loves are dashed, he generalizes his predicament by comparing it to the Seine. For he senses, in the flow of the river,
an allegory of the coming and going of human existence:
"Il lui était indifférent de se perdre dans la mer, car elle
savait qu'elle repasserait entre ces quais, qu'elle regarderait
d'en bas les jambes de ces mêmes ponts et qu'elle reflèterait
de nouveau la pointe de l'île Saint-Louis et les lumières de
la ville."[7]

Jaloux's tendency to envisage reality through the spectrum
of symbols appears most effectively in his transcription of
dreams. We saw that in his novels of the 1920's the author
related the phantasies of his characters and communicated
their semiconscious states. In *La Grenade mordue*, however,
the narrator meticulously describes the dreams of his sleep-
ing hours, in which his beloved appears successively as
the embodiment of ideal beauty, as a furtive ghost, a terrifying medusa, and finally as a pile of dust: "Et l'épouvante
m'éveilla," he remembers "sans me laisser le temps d'aller
jusqu'au bout de mon désir."[8] Claire's metamorphosis thus
symbolizes the inevitable crumbling of Englebert's lifelong
and impassioned hope of possessing her.

Jaloux's vision of his personages as types of human fate
enabled him to endow their mortal life with universal
meaning and to give them an entirely new dimension. The
character of François Englebert exemplifies that archetypal
point of view. Despite the confusion which surrounds his
dreamlike existence, that personage stands out in bold relief.
Unlike Claude Lothaire, the hero of *Les Profondeurs de la
mer*, who fails to acquire a distinct identity, the sensitive
and struggling art critic of *La Grenade mordue* symbolizes

117

man's incapacity to control his fate, or to grasp the infinite complexity of his own nature.

The character of Patrick Séléré likewise conveys the perplexities of a man of delicate feelings confronted with a social order in which traditional values have been swept away. Unlike François Englebert, however, the hero of the novel can articulate in his work his inner conflicts, his anguish and his resentments. In his paintings, Séléré seeks to bring out the soul of the person or the essence of the object that he portrays: "Une oeuvre de Patrick Séléré," exclaims the narrator, "c'est la vie même; et quelque chose de plus que la vie: le mystère qu'elle transporte avec elle, . . ."[9] For the painter is interested mainly in the content of his pictures, rather than in their form, and thus chiefly concerned with the emotion that they communicate.[10] That romantic approach to art serves to isolate Séléré from the abstract tendencies of his time. He experiences, moreover, much difficulty in discovering the salient traits of his models. In the course of that endeavor, he begins to question the very existence of individuality. Little by little he has come to realize that our fundamental passions are not reflected in the physiognomy, but that they appear in the myths which men create and by which they live. These thoughts he expresses to his friends:

En réalité, les choses se passent comme si notre esprit créait des fantômes plus forts que nous et qui nous réduisent en esclavages.... Ceux qui s'aiment deviennent à peu près inconscients et irresponsables de leur propre passion. Mais ils conçoivent un monstre intermédiaire . . . qui les courbe et qui les broie. Tout ce qui est de nous semble se faire hors de nous.[11]

Patrick Séléré's belief that modern man conceivably reincarnates an ancestral type, produces in him a grave crisis of identity. In his search for an understanding of himself, and in the perplexity that he experiences, Séléré is symbolic of the prevailing uncertainty with regard to the meaning of life and of the human fate.

Jaloux, however, reserves the use of myth in *La Grenade mordue* for the leading female character. Thus, the fate of Claire Berger is told through the intermediary of the legend of Persephone. In Greek mythology, that goddess was abducted by the king of the underworld. Persephone's journey through the somber realms of Hades and the rumor that she had tasted of the food of the dead would forever prevent her return among the living.[12] Jaloux, however, transforms that myth into an allegory of the trials of life. It will be recalled that Claire Berger was at one time on the brink of death, from which she was rescued by her two friends. In adapting the ancient myth to the present, Jaloux poses the question whether anyone who has suffered a personal tragedy can ever fully recover his place in the world. The novelist explains his tendency to universalize the individual in an interview with the critic Jean Debrix:

> Pour ce qui est de mon roman *La Grenade mordue*, j'ai été amené à en traiter le sujet par le spectacle, si fréquent dans la vie, de ces êtres qui, après avoir été brisés ou par un trop grand amour, ou par un trop grand chagrin, cessent presque d'agir et d'aimer la vie. Je me suis souvenu à leur propos de Perséphone qui, enlevée par le dieu des enfers, emmenée sous terre et rappelée par sa mère Cérès, ne put jamais redevenir une vraie vivante.[13]

Jaloux's presentation of the ancient myth, however, is completely modern, for he explores the inner consciousness of his character at certain crucial moments. While Claire finds herself in the throes of death, like her prototype who crossed the river Styx, we perceive the hallucinating and confused images that race through her mind. Her life is compared to a fortified city, whose strong walls crumble while she is sliding deeper into unconsciousness. As in a nightmare, the girl attempts to stave off the approach of death by a stealthy escape from the imaginary town. But a phantom pursues her through its winding streets. Occasionally, a woman dressed in a sumptuous robe crosses Claire's path: she is the prospective wife of her own faithless husband. The rapid sequence of these weird images gives the reader a vivid sensation of the chaotic and mysterious passage from life to death. Claire tries to conjure up this scene of horror:

J'ai le souvenir d'une course éperdue à travers des galeries souterraines, de longs couloirs obscurs. Quelqu'un me poursuivait que je sentais haleter derrière moi. Parfois je tombais, et cette horreur sans nom possible allait me sauter dessus. Je me relevais et je me remettais à courir, hésitant aux perpétuelles bifurcations des corridors, allant au hasard à travers les demi-ténèbres, dans une solitude incommensurable....[14]

But if Jaloux has thus clothed the story of Persephone in a modern garb, he has retained the element of fatality that was an essential component of the original Greek myth. The author emphasizes the inevitability of Claire's doom by describing the powerful sway of her instinctive drives. He thus foreshadows the ultimate victory of these forces over her rational self. Though Claire reads, from the beginning, into Malgouyres' faithless character, she is unable, despite the entreaties of her friends, to control her feelings and refuse his proposal. In bringing out Claire's blind compulsion, however, Jaloux does not resort to a minute interpretation of the heroine's patterns of behavior, after the manner of the Freudian analysts. On the contrary, the novelist's portrayal of her inner crisis is essentially poetical, as he transmutes the heroine's feelings into suggestive images:

Si, du fond de son gouffre, Claire distinguait une forme vivante, debout auprès de la barque livide, ... c'était le fantôme de cette Hermine qui avait poussé Claire à la mort. Ce semblant de force s'évanouissait, les harpies de l'autre monde se ruaient vers le nôtre, se hâtaient à leur sombre festin.[15]

We thus become involved in Claire's ordeal through the weird and somber visions that pass haphazardly through her mind. By evoking her nightmares, her obsessive fears, her descent into primeval nothingness, François Englebert suggests the mystery and forlornness of the human spirit in the face of impending death.

In his last novels, Jaloux resorts to his customary device of presenting through the eyes of a narrator the setting in which the characters move. As in his earlier work, the portrayal of the scenery is highly original. But in the novels of this period the visible world in itself seems unimportant; it has become a source of imagery and symbols for the expression of the characters' inner feelings: "Tout me paraissait noir, sordide, mal éclairé," recalls the disillusioned narrator, "les eaux épaisses du fleuve roulaient une huile visqueuse, froide, où flottaient des épaves, des épluchures de vivants, des souliers de morts, des choses rompues."[16] The Stygian darkness of the river, like the haunting landscape of a dream, becomes symbolic of man's loneliness in defeat.

This quest for a subjective and unseen world enables the author to introduce fantastic figures illustrating the various emotions that struggle within the breast of the narrator. For instance, he imagines hearing the voices of four draped figures: Hope, Despair, Love and Poetry. As in Greek drama, these voices intermingle to form a chorus which narrates in poetic form the hero's longings and perplexities. These allegories illustrate also the cycle of birth, growth, senescence and death; indeed the narrator observes the repetition of that cycle in the world of nature. For the circular flow of the Seine's waters suggests to him the eternal process of birth and death, even as the river's onward motion symbolizes the continual reincarnation of the feel-

121

ings and hopes of one generation into the hopes and feelings of the next.

In *La Grenade mordue*, symbol and myth serve to dramatize some of the fundamental issues of life. Such an issue is the impact that a grave misfortune has on the individual person. The knowledge that the characters of this novel derive from life's experience destroys their will to live. The myth that the author adapts in this novel — Persephone's journey to the underworld — therefore becomes symbolic of the fact that knowledge, when it has once been acquired, can never be effaced.

We saw that Edmond Jaloux renewed the myth by shifting the interest from heroism to introspection.[17] For unlike Greek legend, in which the characters express themselves through action, rather than ideas, *La Grenade mordue* exemplifies the yearnings, hesitations and fears which trouble the personages, as we become witnesses to the obscure meanderings of their secret thought. The changes that Jaloux has wrought in the theme of the original story emphasize the modernity of his approach, and they illustrate the final attitude of the novelist. While the Greek legends endow their tragic heroes with an aura of majesty, Jaloux describes his chief protagonists as paltry creatures, shorn of their former pride and dignity. Suffering elevates the spirit of the Greek hero. In Jaloux's novel, however, the injustices of fate reduce the characters to submissiveness and impotence.

By thus bringing out the futility of suffering, Jaloux reflects the doubts and anxieties of his own time, as well as the fatalism of his later years. Moreover, the indiscriminate humbling of the protagonists emphasizes the difference between ancient and modern conceptions of life. While the Greek myths implied the existence of a rational and ordered universe,[18] Jaloux, in adapting them to the contemporary scene, conveys his characters' powerlessness in the face of an unintelligible world. The legends of antiquity tend to show that man is ennobled by the trials he endures, by battling the Furies which the gods have sent against him.[19]

But the sanguine faith in the heroic life as well as the reassuring belief in a divinely ordered universe gave way, during this period, to an apocalyptic vision of chaos and disintegration.[20] The predominance of blind and irrational drives thus came to be regarded as the motivating forces within man and society.

These irrational drives permeate a novel which Jaloux wrote in 1937, entitled *L'Égarée*. That work again reveals the author's interest in the myths of the Greeks. For it is by interpreting ancient legends that he ties together in this novel the various strands of a complicated plot. In *L'Égarée*, however, Jaloux adapts Greek mythology even more freely than in his earlier work. Instead of elaborating on a single theme, he fuses several legends to illustrate some fundamental aspects of the human condition, such as the ambiguities of man's actions, his quest for self-fulfillment, his incapacity to communicate or to achieve desired goals. As we shall see, Jaloux modernizes the ancient myth in order to illuminate the relationship between the various levels of human experience: the worldly and the transcendental, the temporal and the eternal. Again the author adopts some of the surrealist techniques, as he seeks to clarify the fundamental conflicts that pit the sentient individual against a mute and indifferent world. To capture the essence of the person's reality, Jaloux introduces into his narrative startling coincidences, strange events and dreams. In the same vein, he summons up his characters' hallucinations to bring out their involuntary and unconscious states of mind.

In 1937, when Jaloux wrote *L'Égarée*, he was influenced by Edgar Allan Poe, one of his favorite authors since the time of his youth.[21] In composing this novel, Jaloux evoked some of the American writer's principal themes. He drew inspiration from "The Mystery of Marie Rogêt", which tells of an effort to reconstruct from mere facts the disappearance of a girl, but without any success. Jaloux was influenced also by "The Fall of the House of Usher", which describes the wanderings of a young woman's ghost, as it glides through the dark hall of a haunted mansion. The tales of Poe emphasize the elusive character of truth; his personages being shrouded in an atmosphere of terror and opaque mystery. These are also the salient features of this novel, which is replete with drama and suspense.

In choosing the locale for *L'Egarée,* the novelist reverted to his favorite Provence which he had poeticized, we saw, in *Fumées dans la campagne.* This new work illustrates the decline of an aristocratic family in that region. Alfred d'Eymeric de Suffren belongs to the landed nobility, and like many other members of his class, he seeks to unravel the tangled history of his ancestors. He is anxious, therefore, to classify the extensive collection of family papers that has accumulated in the castle over the centuries. To assist him in that task, Suffren recruits a young scholar, Laurent Guelbert. During his stay at the castle, the historian has the opportunity to meet the Suffren family, which is distinguished by its eccentricity. The marquis is a compulsive talker who punctuates his conversation with constant fits of laughter; his son, the unworthy Jean-Baptiste, drowns his ennui in drink and in the hunt. Two daughters, Andrée and Alexandrine, complete that peculiar family.

Alexandrine lives, or rather languishes, in the tower of the castle; her father has confined her there, for he pretends to regard his daughter as insane, and therefore seeks to conceal her alleged disability. But even his ingenious precautions cannot insulate Alexandrine altogether from the outside world. One day, as Guelbert is walking on the estate, he is handed an unsigned letter, asking him to visit the fortress during the night. Intrigued by that singular request, the scholar decides to keep the appointment. As he enters the darkened room, he discovers Alexandrine. Guelbert did not know of Alexandrine's existence; he had anticipated meeting Andrée instead at the nocturnal rendezvous. To allay his curiosity, the captive recounts to the startled visitor an episode from her life. Some years ago, at a ball, she had met a writer and fallen in love with him. Her father and

124

her brother, however, conspired to check the growth of that relationship, and they began to isolate her. Suffren even assigned Magali, a servant, to be his daughter's jailer.

Moved by the girl's pathetic story, Guelbert envisions her as Andromeda chained to a rock, and, like a new Perseus, resolves to engineer her escape. Magali, who loathes her masters, secretly pledges her assistance to Guelbert. On a dark night the threesome unlock the castle gate, and start their journey toward Paris. But the gallant young man has no sooner reached the capital than he grows apprehensive of his future responsibilities. He now begins to regret the generous impulse that had incited him to liberate the girl. Sensing the young man's growing coolness toward her, Alexandrine decides to leave him, and sets out to find her former suitor. However, the icy reception of the latter chills her to the marrow. Forlorn and without hope, Alexandrine throws herself in a river, whose swift currents engulf her. In the meanwhile, Suffren had left his estate for Paris, in quest of the missing couple. When he finally meets Guelbert, he learns of his daughter's tragic death. In this moment of supreme trial, the master of Eymeric fully reveals his callousness. Far from showing sorrow, Suffren declares in even voice that his daughter's suicide merely confirmed that she was insane. On hearing these words, Magali, who had faithfully tended Alexandrine to the end, broke out into uncontrolled wailing. Of all those who had known the girl, only a servant possessed the humanity and the elemental feeling to grasp in its fullness the horror of Alexandrine's fate.

In *L'Egarée*, Edmond Jaloux introduces a new approach to the setting. His previous novel of myth and symbol contained sceneries that were largely allegoric: the notion of eternal life was associated with the Seine, Paris in the spring illustrated nature's vitality, its magic and precariousness. However, in the novel that we are now considering, the environment becomes symbolic of preternatural and unseen forces; surroundings no longer represent abstract

125

thought. The ghostlike castle of Eymeric is shrouded in a sea of mystery that conveys the novel's sense of terror. Bathed, now in a pale candlelight, now in the shadows of evening, the castle's tower inevitably brings to mind the eerie figure of Alexandrine. Similarly the author's description of the mistral, howling through the branches of the castle's pine forest, suggests the madness of the lonely woman imprisoned in her own fears, and doing her utmost to break out of her bondage:

> On regardait au passage des bois, pareils à des sanctuaires béants, où, de-ci, de-là, une haute pierre blanche se disposait à recevoir un sacrifice. Des rondes de branches obéissaient aux tourbillons du vent.... Les têtes de cyprès aux gaines noires se penchaient et s'échevelaient à la façon d'un cheval sauvage qui affronte une tempête.[22]

In applying that method of establishing a parallel between the characters of the novel and their surroundings, Jaloux reveals once more the extent of his debt to Edgar Allan Poe.[23]

But if the novelist now conjures up a weird and fantastic scenery, his description of that scenery is almost realistic in its exhaustiveness. As Léon Daudet tersely remarked: "Jaloux nous montre Alexandrine tenue à l'écart dans un milieu provincial, merveilleusement, minutieusement décrit."[24] Thus he depicts minutely the various architectural styles that coexist in the castle of Eymeric. In the attention that he lavishes on detail, the author goes so far as to portray the arabesque carvings which adorn the main staircase. This very precise rendering of an essentially imaginary setting intensifies for the reader the mood of horror and of dread that Jaloux now seeks to convey.

In presenting the characters of *L'Egarée*, Jaloux continues to bring together the individual and his prototype by identifying the ephemeral person with a mythical hero. This association of the particular and the transcendent orders, which enables the novelist to illustrate different levels of consciousness, is a technique that Jaloux applies tellingly in drawing the portrait of Laurent Guelbert. When that personage is driven by an instinctive reaction to liberate the captive girl, he fancies himself, we saw, to be another Perseus, who rescues Andromeda from the perils that endanger her life. Jaloux, however, empties the ancient myth of its heroic content, for he shows that Guelbert's desire to free the prisoner was motivated unconsciously by the will to gain complete mastery over her: "Il désirait obtenir d'Alexandrine un corps moins défendu, plus humilié encore que les autres... parce qu'il serait le seul vers lequel elle se tournerait avec dévotion et reconnaissance."[25] Guelbert's obsession with a woman, as abandoned as Andromeda chained to her cliff, reveals his sensual temperament. Unlike the hero of *La Grenade mordue* whose exalted love for Claire Berger drove his passion into the realm of unconscious dreams, Guelbert's veneer of chivalry hardly conceals his erotic desires.

Jaloux thus modernizes the Greek myth by analyzing the workings of the mind and the motivations underlying human conduct. In the ancient myth, Perseus at no time was assailed by doubt, as he performed his labors for the rescue of Andromeda. However, in Jaloux's contemporary rendering of that myth, the fear of laying himself open to ridicule always intervenes and dampens the protagonist's ardor in the pursuit of his goal. It is particularly after Guelbert's arrival in Paris with Alexandrine that the image of a fearless new Perseus is badly tarnished. For Guelbert is now afraid of the opinion of his friends, thus proving himself a fainthearted conformist.[26] Jaloux is showing, therefore, that modern man deceives himself when he believes that he is emulating the ancient heroes. In following the myth of Perseus, Laurent Guelbert is really escaping from his more authentic, and unheroic self.

If Guelbert is a weak and unstable man, the character

of Alexandrine emerges as a striking figure, standing out in bold relief against the dismal background of the castle of Eymeric. In creating the leading female character, Jaloux again adapts the classical legends to modern times. Alexandrine, who yearns for her freedom, personifies the Greek heroine Andromeda. Like her archetype, she displays an unshakable loyalty toward her rescuer, despite her father's tyrannical opposition to all human contact. In *L'Egarée*, however, Jaloux takes more freedom with the myths, combining the characteristics of several ancient figures to complete the portrait and thus to heighten its tragic meaning.[27]

In her own cloistered personality, Alexandrine reveals traits of such mythical personages as Medusa and Cassandra. Of the first-named figure, Alexandrine possesses a number of physical features, particularly the faraway look of her phosphorescent eyes, and her disheveled hair. "Elle secouait les boucles de sa chevelure, qui se tordaient comme les serpents de Gorgone. Pour un peu, Laurent eût cru que ses cheveux allaient siffler."[28] From the latter, she adopted the passionate and sensual nature, as well as a congenital incapacity to convince others of the veracity of her prophecies. For she often expressed her premonition of an untoward end. Moreover, the unhappy Alexandrine, unable to communicate with others, slowly wasting away and held to be mad, evokes the tragic figure of Cassandra.

In drawing on the legendary Greek tales, Jaloux now shows an interest chiefly in the theme of fatalism. This theme, which dominated the life of Claire Berger, also rules Alexandrine's lonely existence. But Claire's jealousy and her yearning for death manifested themselves in the terrifying images of her nightmares; Alexandrine's forebodings on the other hand spring from her own interpretation of everyday experiences. The act of crushing a butterfly, for instance, releases all her fears and ingrained sense of guilt: "— Je me suis persuadée que j'avais tué autre chose qu'un papillon," she confesses, "je ne sais quoi, une espèce d'esprit et qu'il me poursuivait de sa vengeance."[29] Similarly, the breaking of a glass fills her with anguish, the grating noise of the falling pieces having brought out, momentarily the primitive chaos of an enigmatic world. In the last stages of his evolution as a writer, Jaloux would thus emphasize the ineluctability of man's fate.

If Alexandrine is symbolic of such fatality, her profound faith in the value of individual conscience, which impels her to unmask the surrounding hypocrisy, makes her an unforgettable character. During her seclusion, Alexandrine is a poignant figure, as she struggles alone against her father's wanton scheme to represent her as insane. The fact that her opinions are sharply at variance with the conventional wisdom of society, serves also to bring out her distinctive personality. Alexandrine illustrates, above all, the isolation of the individual in a harsh and friendless world. When the hope that she had nurtured throughout her captivity of finding rapture in some emotional experience crumbles, she feels locked in a life-and-death struggle against the hostility of people and of things: "Elle eut, pour la première fois depuis son départ d'Eymeric, le sentiment d'avoir échappé à la sécurité et à la sauvegarde pour entrer en lutte avec le monde hostile."[30] The anguish that grips her is so overpowering that she can no longer oppose the breakdown of her rationality, or react against the fatality of her doom. Because she is defenseless and utterly alone in her defeat, Alexandrine is one of the most moving of all the characters that appear in the world of fiction of Edmond Jaloux.

It was Jaloux's concern with the fundamental meaning of human destiny that explains his interest in Greek myths as well as his belief in their perennial youthfulness. In *La Grenade mordue*, we saw, the author made use of the legend of Persephone in order to demonstrate the shattering impact of a great misfortune on a delicate and sensitive woman. But he modernizes the myth by withdrawing it from the realm of the gods and by applying it exclusively to the world of man. Claire Berger's transformation from a merely

129

suspicious wife into a morbidly jealous woman, bent on suicide, reenacts, as it were, Persephone's terrifying passage across the river Styx. In the original myth, Persephone's recurrent voyages from the underworld to earth symbolized man's need to come to terms with life and death.[31] However, in Jaloux's renewal of the legend, the leading protagonist has lost by her experience of tragedy all desire to return among the living.

In *L'Egarée*, Jaloux continues to use the ancient legends as a parable of certain fundamental problems of the human condition. Thus, he elucidates altruistic as well as selfish aspects of a generous act by reviving the tale of Perseus and Andromeda. In this work, however, Jaloux no longer confines himself to the meaning of a single myth, as he had done in *La Grenade mordue;* he now incorporates a number of ancient themes in the central story on which the novel is based. The leading character of *L'Egarée* is not patterned exclusively on Andromeda. Alexandrine de Suffren, by the very harshness of her fate, also resembles Cassandra. Like the Trojan seer, she possesses the ability to foretell her destiny; like her archetype, Alexandrine produces only a reaction of disbelief whenever she engages in prophecy. However, when Jaloux evoked the myth of Cassandra, he sought above all to exemplify the truth that society brands as mad and places outside of its pale those who feel compelled by an overpowering urge to issue forecasts of tragedy. The author's almost exclusive dependence on Greek mythology during this philosophical phase of his career was due to the conviction of his later years that man cannot escape the working out of his fate.[32]

Jaloux often departs, as we saw, from the original Greek myths. Unlike the ancient heroes, his protagonists are not ennobled by the trials and sufferings that they undergo. The characters of his last novels in reality glide past our eyes like shadows in a meaningless universe. But the novelist does not regenerate his personages through revolt, as the existentialists would do. He is content to dissipate the som-

130

berness that permeates his last works by entwining his leading characters in the poetical aura of the legends of ancient Greece.

CHAPTER VIII

THE NOVELS OF MYSTICAL EXPERIENCE

During the 1930's, we saw, Edmond Jaloux sought primarily to bring out in his work the universal significance of the inner life through the modernization of some of mankind's oldest and most representative myths. His search for the meaning of human experience, though it took place in the rarefied atmosphere of abstruse symbols, did not, however, insulate the author from everyday life. His novels of that period at no time lacked a definite locale, and they were never without a specific point in time. While the characters of these works personify universal traits, they nevertheless retain distinct personalities, which stand revealed by an analysis in depth.

The late 1930's witnessed the advent of a new phase in the evolution of Edmond Jaloux as a novelist that was also to be his last. The author moved to Switzerland on the eve of World War II.[1] There, far from the literary polemics of the French capital, he wrote several novels that reflect his spiritual alienation from the contemporary world.[2] The most important of these books are *Le Culte secret* (1941) *Le Pays des fantômes* (1948), and the still unpublished work "La Pêche aux flambeaux." These three novels reveal a number of common features that differentiate them sharply from the novels of myth and symbol of the preceding period. For in the works of his last phase, Edmond Jaloux strove to unlock the gates of the extrasensory world instead of projecting the inner life of his personages, as he had done in his fiction of the early 1930's.

In pursuing his mystical quest, Edmond Jaloux might seem at first sight to be veering further away from the

132

predominant tendencies of French literature in the 1940's. The guiding spirits of that time questioned the very meaning of existence and thus advocated involvement in the larger struggle against the forces of absurdity. For existentialism was expounding a new philosophy of human action stressing the individual's responsibility to his fellow men, his total freedom, his need to resist oppression. Existentialism, which expressed the mood of anxiety that pervaded the war years, seemed to be exerting an unchallenged influence over French thought. Its impact had indeed been so far-reaching that it succeeded in overshadowing a number of parallel currents. Simultaneously with the doctrines of Sartre and Camus, a movement flourished that concerned itself primarily with spiritual experience.[3] The leading figures of that tendency were the Belgians Franz Hellens and Henri Michaux, and the Frenchman Julien Gracq.[4]

These novelists create a universe of pure phantasy by reflecting the outside world exclusively through their characters' fears and premonitions. Their fiction is suffused with hallucinating images that reduce concrete reality to insignificance. By thus obliterating the distinction between the seen and the unseen, these writers leave one wondering about the very existence of the environment that surrounds us. Such works as Hellens' *Nouvelles Réalités fantastiques* (1941), Michaux's *Voyage en Grande Garabagne* (1936) and Gracq's *Au château d'Argol* (1938) convey the uncertainty of man's relation to an enigmatic universe, as well as the modern anxiety with its obsession of chaos and of nothingness. Jaloux's last novels are clearly part of this visionary movement, which developed at the same time as existentialism.

Le Culte secret, a novel which Jaloux wrote on the eve of World War II, was his first work that revealed this spiritualistic trend. That novel may be regarded as transitional in form and revolutionary in substance. Its theme is closely related to the mysticism that flourished before and during the war; it is pervaded by the motif of death and by the idea of the supernatural. On the one hand the theme of death manifests itself through the sway which the departed continue to exert over the living; the idea of the supernatural, on the other hand, becomes apparent through the characters' possession of occult powers, a faculty that enables them to cast spells and foretell the future. The narrative technique of *Le Culte secret,* however, is still closely patterned on the novels of Jaloux's period of myth and symbol, thus assigning to it a place midway between the novels of myth and those of his mystical period.

The quest for an invisible world and the theme of death are the twin threads with which the action of that novel is woven. *Le Culte secret* traces the history of two noble families, the Draceynac and the Courvalgrelot of which the latter resides in Paris and the former in the Quercy. Jean de Draceynac, the hero of the novel, is orphaned at an early age. Jean's father, having banished the thought of a remarriage, entrusts his son to the care of farmers dwelling on his estate. These country folk live close to nature; they are ingenuous and filled with a sense of awe before life's mysteries. They are imbued also with the idea that man cannot escape a just retribution for evil deeds — a result that they attribute to the mysterious workings of incantation. In the course of his upbringing, Jean absorbs the same sense of the mystery of life that pervades the spiritual existence of his guardians.

As an adolescent, Jean was sent to Paris in order to begin his formal education. His stay in the capital brought him into contact with one of his late mother's relatives, Henri de Courvalgrelot and his wife Catherine. Theirs was a thoroughly ill-sorted match. Henri was an ascetic, leading a rigidly ordered life, while Catherine loved freedom and adventure. That marriage drove the impulsive Catherine to loathing her over-punctilious husband. Henri, for his part, was unable either to fulfill his wife's deeper yearnings or to reform his ways. But these disabilities in no way lessened his affection for Catherine. His unrequited love, however,

134

aroused in him an overwhelming desire for the demise of his wife. For in death, Henri could at last possess unscathed the recollection of his love, as his feelings toward Catherine had always borne a remote and disembodied character. He now proceeded to transform his *hôtel* into a sanctuary, dedicated to his wife's memory, and preserving it down to the least significant object in the exact order in which it lay at the time of her death.

Jean de Draceynac displays a similar loyalty to a dead love, and a like morbid strain as his cousin Henri. On reaching manhood, he had married Laurence de Silézune, a distant relative of his family. His marriage also came to a premature end when his wife died in childbirth. Jean experienced that event as a trauma, for it released in him all of the fears of the supernatural that he had acquired in childhood, under the tutelage of the farmers on his estate. Haunted by the idea that the souls of the dead cast a spell over the living, Jean, like his cousin Henri, worshiped the memory of his wife. However in him that cult of the dead proved to be ephemeral. The arrival of Laurence's sister in his estate exorcised the ghostly spirit of his departed wife, and turned his gaze away from the nocturnal vision to the luminous vista of life.

In developing the theme of the relation between the living and the dead, and in emphasizing the preeminence of unseen worlds, Edmond Jaloux was influenced chiefly by the mystical vision of two abstruse poets: Milosz and Rilke.[5] The poetry of Milosz abounds in funeral images, in descriptions of cemeteries and tombstones. These objects serve to introduce the reader into the silent realm of the dead. In *Les Sept Solitudes*, Milosz summons up the world of the hereafter which he portrays as a refuge from the travail of earthly life. The spirits who sail through that Elysian domain seem to the poet to be more alive than the living, who dwell in an opaque world of appearances, and are thus subject to perpetual delusion.

If Milosz gave Edmond Jaloux a poetical vision of the

135

hereafter, it was Rilke's discovery of new shores beyond the frontiers of earthly life that suggested the main themes of *Le Culte secret* and *Le Pays des fantômes*. Rilke's *Duino Elegies* enlarge the scope of human experience by fusing the worldly with the otherworldly aspects of human experience. His *Sonnets to Orpheus*, which carry on a protracted quest for a transcendent reality, influenced Jaloux in the last phase of his development as a novelist of mystical experience.

Jaloux's growing involvement with the occult also affected his creation of characters, as well as his choice of a setting. That new tendency becomes fully apparent when we compare the archetypes of his earlier novels of myth to the ethereal personages of his last period. While the leading characters in *La Grenade mordue* and *l'Egarée* incarnated fundamental aspects of the human fate, the protagonists of *Le Culte secret* have presentiments of undying powers that invisibly affect the life of man. Instead of representing ideas, as they had in his earlier works, these personages have been transformed into seekers of the unknown. But in analyzing family background and upbringing to explain their mystical bent, the novelist mingles rational and enigmatic elements, making *Le Culte secret* a stage in Jaloux's evolution toward pure phantasy.

Thus, in the early chapters of this book, we see the bleak ancestral castle in which Jean de Draceynac spent his first years, and we become acquainted with the superstitious peasant women who were charged with his upbringing. "Je connus très vite le folklore du pays," recalled Draceynac in his later years, "j'appris aussi à avoir foi dans les miracles, à préférer le hasard à la logique."[6] From the very beginning we get an inkling, therefore, of the character's inclination toward visionary experience. The period that Jean spent in Paris reinforces his imaginative bent. Recoiling from the artificiality and smugness of urban society, the young provincial withdraws into a dream world of his own that foreshadows his ultimate receptivity to mysticism. Moreover the ghastly murder of the young man's father in the forest of Draceynac and the suicide of his cousin Catherine, who in his eyes epitomized ideal womanhood, intensify his susceptibility to extrasensory experience. For these successive deaths bring with them a revelation of the transitoriness of our physical life, and thus prompt him to transcend the limitations of earthly existence.[7]

In his protracted quest after unseen worlds, Jean de Draceynac begins by searching himself. Conflicting pressures, however, struggle within his consciousness. Against life's shortness, he seeks solace in a spiritual reality. And yet, Jean is unwilling to desist from life's gratifications. The clash of these two tendencies within him explain the shortness of his trips into imaginary worlds, and thus his frequent returns to everyday reality.[8]

For all their brevity, Jean's mystical experiences are of two kinds. One consists in a pantheistic union with nature, the other in a hallucinating vision that entails a swift succession of bizarre images, representing the whole spectrum of the human condition. The following description is illustrative of the mood that invariably leads the character to a supernatural union with nature:

> C'est le soir. Des ombres fabuleuses plongent dans le Tarn, comme si elles allaient procéder à je ne sais quel solennel baptême; ou bien elles y font descendre des seaux profonds qu'elles en ramènent tout ruisselants d'étoiles et d'eau. Tout ce qui est indistinct se peuple de majestueuses présences.[9]

As he watches the flow of that river, Jean gradually loses his feeling of isolation and becomes part of the stream, as if he were transformed into a sea anemone.[10] Elsewhere, while observing the stars in a moonlit sky, he perceives a series of fantastic visions that conjure up with stunning realism the great variety of the works of man. These images, which convey to Jean de Draceynac a panoramic view of human endeavor, also give him that otherworldly feeling in

137

which all things become translucent. But these experiences are fleeting and infrequent: "Cette rêverie, où des images étranges s'entrechoquaient et se bousculaient devant mes yeux . . . avait duré à peine quelques secondes," he remembered after awakening from his mystical rapture into the world of familiar sounds and sites.[11]

Jaloux's evolution towards mysticism also manifests itself in his portrayal of the hero's cousin, Catherine de Courvalgrelot. For she no longer resembles the prototypes of the novels of myth and symbol. The leading characters of such works as *La Grenade mordue* and *L'Egarée* illustrated, as we saw, an essential truth about the human condition.[11a] That archetypal quality has disappeared in the works of the last period. The theme of death, which in Jaloux's earlier fiction was indissolubly linked to a tragic fate, has now been transformed into a search for an invisible world.

In portraying Catherine's need to communicate with the hereafter, Jaloux brings out the rational as well as the mystical aspects of a person's spiritual journey. The heroine's cult of a deceased friend, her fruitless search for his tomb, her realization that his memory has faded all speak to her of the lurking presence of death. "Je ne sentis pas Catherine à demi défaillante sous le poids d'un secret ou d'une tristesse particulière," sadly remarks the narrator.[12] For he now realizes that it was the fear of this shadow that kindled in her an intense desire to escape from the oppressive world of doubt into the quiet realm of the dead."Ce désir de la mort," as Jaloux observes "n'est sans doute pas autre chose que le besoin d'échapper à l'angoisse que son ombre fait peser sur les hommes."[13] While this portrait reveals new mystical overtones, it retains nevertheless the dual vision — logical and supernatural — a vision that proves once more the transitional nature of this novel.

Of all the characters in *Le Culte secret*, Henri de Courvalgrelot is the most unfathomable. When we compare him with the personages of the novels of myth and symbol, it becomes evident that Jaloux's method of characterization has evolved from simple to highly complex forms. In *L'Egarée* and *La Grenade mordue* Jaloux singled out a predominant trait, in order to emphasize the symbolic meaning of his archetypal figures. Thus, we saw that François Englebert, the art critic in *La Grenade mordue*, illustrates the loneliness of the idealist in a materialistic world.[14] The heroes of Jaloux's last novels, however, stand revealed through an unraveling of their hidden desires, and their search for mystical experience is too abstruse to exemplify a general truth about human nature. If the characters now cease to represent a specific aspect of the human fate, this is due to the fact that Jaloux in his last years communicated to these personages his own thirst for a transcendent and immortal world.

The hero of *Le Culte secret*, for example, seeks above all to free himself from the restrictions of time and space. His quest for ultimate truth is inextricably bound up with his peculiar relationship toward his wife. We saw that Henri was frustrated in his love. That failure intensified his passion and drives him into a search for a mystical union with Catherine, completely independent of physical contact.[14a] Catherine's untimely death marks the beginning of Henri's retrospective journey into the silent realm of his own recollections. Having transformed his house into an abode of his wife's phantom, he lives in a timeless world of dream:

> Dans la maison d'Henri les laques, les porcelaines chinoises, les effigies de mandarins gardaient leur place habituelle, mais le temps avait comme amorti leurs angles, atténué les couleurs . . . Une odeur très vieille, une odeur d'épices orientales et de myrrhe, s'exhalait des pièces, qui semblaient plus grandes, mais où la lumière entrait moins. On y rencontrait peu de monde et l'on ne sentait pas la présence du temps entre ces murailles vaguement dorées.[15]

Henceforth he dedicates himself to the cult of his dead love with the single-mindedness of a religious votary. Wholly

139

impervious to everyday reality, Henri has thus become a true mystic. The fulfillment of his quest sets the stage for the triumph of pure phantasy in the last novel of Edmond Jaloux.

When he created the setting of *Le Culte secret,* the author fused imaginative elements, such as he had already employed in earlier novels, with supernatural ones that likewise foreshadow the scenery of his last work. We saw that in the course of his evolution as a writer Edmond Jaloux gradually substituted photographic descriptions with subjective portrayals. He continued that trend in *Le Culte secret.* In conjuring up the forest at Draceynac, for instance, the author gives a free rein to his imagination. He personifies the trees and makes them so suggestive of the human form as to evoke nature's threatening forces and its primeval mystery.

> Les arbres trapus, massifs, comme enfoncés dans leur tronc, bossués de loupes énormes, veloutés de lichen, contractés et hargneux se tassaient sur eux-mêmes, jetaient en l'air leur bras musculeux, s'armaient contre Dieu.[16]

A field of wheat swaying in the wind conjures up another original image: "Tout ondulait; cela faisait penser à la brusque reptation d'un immense dragon d'or qui plongeait et se redressait partout presque en même temps."[17] In the 1920's Jaloux had used highly personal imagery and the blending of sense stimuli to suggest relationships between the characters' moods and their surroundings.[18] In his more recent portrayals of the outer world, however, the multifarious manifestations of nature have now become portents of an invisible world. The rustling of the foliage in the stillness of the night and the shimmering of the trees, reflecting the silvery hues of the moon, are described to evoke these unseen realms.[19]

The frequent recurrence of nocturnal sceneries as a setting is another characteristic which announces the ultimate triumph of the visionary element in Edmond Jaloux's evolution as a novelist. The author evokes that impression of darkness through the narrator's vivid recollection of the Draceynac forest and of its mournful castle: "J'errais dans une sorte de sépulcre, tout ouaté de tapisseries, tout assombri de boiseries anciennes."[20] The prevalence of somber colors in this novel is, moreover, closely connected with the theme of death. Jaloux develops that subject by summoning up a faraway country, the land of the departed, whose ghostly spirits are oblivious to the passage of time. The novelist's preoccupation with the subject of death forecasts his emphasis on the supernatural in his last novels. Though he continued in *Le Culte secret* to employ the techniques of his period of poetic imagination, that work already anticipates the author's desire to transcend the limitations of space and time that would typify the final stage of his artistic development.

While the setting of *Le Culte secret* fuses concrete and fantastic elements, the locale of *Le Pays des fantômes* is conveyed in an exclusively poetic and supernatural manner. As we will see, the scenery in this novel no longer represents a concrete place, but evokes a dreamlike and otherworldly atmosphere. The characters of *Le Pays des fantômes* also reveal striking differences from those of the novels of myth and symbol. They are no longer recognizable people, but appear as ghosts returning with extraordinary knowledge from the realm of the dead.

The plot of *Le Pays des fantômes* seems at first sight to be patterned on real life. Two men, one the son and the other the friend of an artist, fall in love with his model, the beautiful Edla Anderson. Edla is attracted to the two young men. But Tony Brussol, the artist's friend, wins her hand by his persistence, by looking for her into the far-off regions of her native Finland. Jean Craisac seeks temporary relief from his disappointment as a naval officer plying the Far Eastern route. Having spent several years in these distant travels, Craisac returns to France, and succeeds in

141

weaning away from Brussol the woman he never ceased to love. Craisac's wanderlust, however, soon drives him back to sea. The abandoned Edla becomes ill. In her plight she begs her estranged husband to take her back. He accedes to her wish. But the resumption of their marriage is short-lived, as Edla dies within a few months of their reconciliation. Seeking to retrieve the recollection of his wife, and also the remembrance of his youth, Brussol returns to the artist's studio, where he first fell in love with Edla. There he suddenly perceives Edla's ghost, and also the spirit of Craisac and of his artist-friend. As he converses with these disembodied spirits he learns that they have discovered the vanity of all earthly passions, and the innocuousness of tragedy when viewed under the aegis of eternity.

This purely imaginative and mystical novel reveals the unmistakable influence of Henrik Ibsen and Knut Hamsun. The development of the two principal themes of this work: the relationship between the living and the dead, and the quest for the meaning of life, owes much to Ibsen's last play, *When We Dead Awaken*.[21] In this drama Ibsen contrasts two opposing views of existence. One, held by a young couple who descends into the valley, regards comfort as the essence of life; the other is illustrated by an aging artist and his former model who climb a mountain in a blinding snowstorm. Both are killed by an avalanche. But their ghosts rise to inhabit the silent mountain tops. In Ibsen's eyes their steep and upward struggle represents the triumph of life over death.

If the supernatural theme of *Le Pays des fantômes* bears the stamp of the mysticism of Ibsen's later years, the eerie landscapes of this novel inevitably recall the nature scenes of Hamsun's *Wanderers*.[22] The originality of that author's descriptions of nature consists in his ability to communicate through direct sense impressions the awesome mystery and weirdness of nature. For Hamsun suggests, through a strange mingling of pantheism and animism, that the soul of man is often a reincarnation of the life of a flower, a plant or a tree.

Like the Norwegian writer, Edmond Jaloux in this novel identifies himself completely with nature. While the settings in his earlier works attached themselves to a given locale, the decor of *Le Pays des fantômes* appears as a timeless Elysian world situated in the subconscious, rather than as a specific place. This new scenery reflects the feelings of the characters as they recall their impressions of the luminous summers in the Finnish lake country. In the imagination of Tony Brussol, the wind whining through the forest has the sound of the music of the heavenly spheres: "Il y avait dans l'air une sonorité inexplicable qui semblait venir de très loin, une sonorité sourde et vibrante qui serrait le coeur comme la rumeur d'un autre monde."[23] Similarly, the remembrance of past springtimes and of the midnight sun brings to Edla's mind intimations of an invisible and eternal world. "L'air qu'on respire est comme de l'éther; on a l'impression d'être entrée dans l'éternité."[24]

Jaloux's evolution towards a purely imaginative setting manifests itself also in the importance that he now attaches to his characters' subconscious. Weird images of translucent objects have become part of the novel's scenery, and they convey a gripping impression of a supernatural world:

Tony venait soudain de poser les doigts sur un bouton glacé de porte. Il secouait fiévreusement une poignée qui lui résistait. De grands espaces lisses filaient sous ses yeux, comme des miroirs dépolis. Parfois, ils reflétaient des images bizarres, des têtes posées sur de larges pierres, des fleurs qui regardaient avec des prunelles élastiques. Et la boutique fut énorme devant lui. Tout était à vendre. Des objets inconnus, magnétiques, divers, scintillants comme l'agate des billes, comme le cristal des carafes. Ils étaient rangés sur des étagères se superposant indéfiniment . . . De nouveau, la vitrine glissa, devint une surface miroitante et polie, et Tony s'aperçut qu'il traversait une région d'étangs ou plutôt, à perte de vue, il n'y avait qu'un lac immense coupé par des ponts de pierre blanche, très ouvragés, qui se croisaient et formaient au-dessus de l'eau une géométrie irrégulière.[25]

As in a dream, the character has the impression that he is gliding stealthily over strange and unknown regions.

The author's progress towards a deeply inward vision of the setting appears most tellingly in the last pages of *Le Pays des fantômes*. The gardens, houses and streets seem ostensibly to be situated in Marseilles. In the novel they belong in fact to an otherworldly realm of gliding spirits and shadows. "(Tony) se dirigea vers le jardin Michel-Ange. Rien ne l'étonnait plus. Il savait bien que le monde, tel qu'il nous apparaît dans la plus grande partie de notre vie, n'est pas tout à fait le vrai. L'un est beaucoup plus vaste; l'autre est moins absurde."[26]

The blurring of the distinction between the worlds of the living and of the dead, that is characteristic of the setting of *Le pays des fantômes*, applies also to the delineation of the characters in this novel. Its personages differ from all the others in Jaloux's fictional work owing to the fact that they are not tied to a concrete milieu, or specific social class. Rather they personify some fundamental attitude that is wholly unrelated to the accident of heredity, education or psychological make-up. This new approach to characterization makes the protagonists emblematic of such divergent philosophies as spiritualism, materialism, or nihilism.

The development from a personal to an emblematic characterization may be observed in the three principal characters of *Le Pays des fantômes*. Thus, the mute hero, Tony Brussol, is no longer a distinct individual. His life is wholly dominated by a quest for perfection, that he seeks above all in physical union. In order to endow his personage with elemental force, Jaloux adopts a new method of characterization. He portrays the hero's longing after the woman he loves through dreamlike visions of an ethereal world, and through imaginary conversations with phantoms. It will be recalled that, in the novels of myth and symbol, Jaloux had already revealed the strange images of his characters' dreams to illustrate their innermost traits and desires. However, during that period, the author drew a sharp line between the realms of dream and of everyday reality.[27] In *Le Pays des fantômes*, that barrier has vanished. Brussol moves indiscriminately between these two worlds without being able to separate them. "Avait-il vraiment rêvé la nuit précédente? Mais si cette scène n'était pas un rêve, que se passait-il donc dans le monde"? the author queries.[28] The Finnish countryside casts such a magic spell over Brussol, that he can no longer tell the seasons from one another, nor differentiate life from death: "Comment séparer ainsi la vie de la mort, l'hiver du printemps, la racine de la fleur?"[29] Finally, when Brussol, as an old man, remembers his departed friends, he wonders once more about his own essence: "Suis-je vivant," he asks, "ou suis-je mort moi-même?"[30]

The occult forces which constantly intervene in the life of Brussol, have even greater impact on the description of Edla Anderson, the leading female personage. For Jaloux's presentation of Edla as a dazzling apparition rather than as a character of flesh and blood, emphasizes her mysteriousness: "Qui êtes-vous petit être silencieux et grave, qui avez toujours l'air de prêter l'oreille à une parole que personne n'entend?" asks her spellbound lover.[31] From the very outset she appears as a luminous being, a seer of the invisible, a person receptive to otherworldly influences.

Not limited by the restrictions of class or environment, Edla personifies womanhood: gentleness and communion with nature. Thus, her recollection of the northern Finnish scenery, where the midnight sun gives the forests and lakes an iridescent glow throughout the summer, arouses in her a feeling for the permanence of light and a sense of eternity: "Les jours étaient interminables dans cette étrange survie du soleil qui exalte les nerfs et qui laisse entrevoir l'infini."[32] Such words as "interminable," "survie" and "infini" all suggest the existence of an invisible and supernatural world. Indeed, when Edla finally reappears as a spirit, she establishes a relationship of harmony with the ghosts of the two men who had loved her, and with whom, when they were still on earth, her own self was so closely, and sometimes so painfully intertwined.

The third major character in this novel, Jean Craisac, a swaggering naval officer, stands in sharp contrast to the diffident and brooding hero. At first sight, Craisac seems to be out of place in an essentially mystical novel. However, by opposing an insensitive person to a man of feeling, Jaloux gives to this work an esthetic as well as an intellectual symmetry. Unlike the other personages who, during their stay on earth, cling nostalgically to the past, Craisac values only the present. Always eager for new experiences, he is unhampered by the recollection of earlier modes of action. "Il ne faut pas voir en moi quelqu'un qui aurait un sentiment très vif du passé," he tells Edla, "je sais trop ce qu'il en coûte de tourner toujours le dos à ce qui nous entoure."[33] But even though he rejects all transcendental values, his spirit, like that of the other personages, rises after death. Thus, he returns as a ghost, and lives in peace with his former rival, as well as with the woman whom he had loved at one time in real life.

By fusing the concrete with the abstract in an incongruous way, Jaloux once more manifests his attachment, even in his mystical period, to a balancing of the physical with the spiritual aspects of life. Throughout his work, the novelist had sought to blend these disparate elements in order to achieve a truly meaningful reconstruction of human experience. It was, in fact, the author's quest for a total grasp of life, and also his search for a transcendental world, which led him toward a mystical conception of the novel during his last phase. His emphasis in the works of that period on the occult distinguishes them from his earlier fiction, in which personages and scenery belonged altogether to the world of visible reality. *Le Culte secret,* with its blending of fact and fancy, marks a transition between poetic imagination and mysticism. But it is only in *Le Pays des fantômes,* where the characters appear alternately as earthly and supernatural beings, that Jaloux's evolution toward spiritualism has reached its final stage. The interlacing of the natural and the supernatural endows his last novel with a magic quality that heightens our interest in the unfathomed aspects of man's relation to himself and to the universe.

CONCLUSION

Having traced Edmond Jaloux's varied and prolific career, which spanned the crucial years between the end of the nineteenth century and the Second World War, we can evaluate his position in modern French literature, and also summarize the main results of our study. An appraisal of the successive stages of this writer's literary life is all the more required in view of the fact that critics who were Jaloux's contemporaries, and by no means unfriendly toward him, lacked an over-all perspective on his development as a novelist.

Such leading commentators as Francis de Miomandre, Henri de Régnier and Benjamin Crémieux viewed Jaloux's evolution essentially as an alternation between realism and imagination.[1] In swinging from one extreme to another, these critics averred, Jaloux was attempting to conciliate two opposite facets of his artistic personality. But they were mistaken in that belief. An attentive examination of Jaloux's career reveals a sequential development from an almost slavish adhesion to the norms of realism in his youth to the freest use of phantasy in his later years. Moreover, imagination did not constitute for Edmond Jaloux an antidote to the photographic realism of his early work. Nor did he alternate between these opposing styles in order to conciliate his own contradictory tendencies. In fact, Jaloux's evolution as a novelist involved a continuous quest for the essence of reality, and a protracted effort to convey it in esthetic form. His vision of the world changed, and as it was transformed, his method and technique also underwent a profound modification. Jaloux's experiments with different approaches to his art, each of which manifests a deeper appreciation on his part of human experience, actu-

148

ally mark the various stages of his growth as a novelist.

We can distinguish six separate periods in Jaloux's fictional works. During his initial phase of development which extends from 1901 to 1906, the novelist strove to reproduce with minute precision the provincial milieu of Marseilles in which he was born and bred, as he faithfully conformed to the literary doctrine of such regional novelists as Ferdinand Fabre and René Boylesve, who exemplified the close interrelationships that existed between man and his environment. In the works of his youth, Jaloux adopted the positivist tendencies of these authors as he sought primarily to portray the acquisitive ethos and the narrow-mindedness of Marseilles' bourgeoisie. Like his immediate predecessors, he emphasized during that period the effect of environmental conditions on the individual. If Jaloux dwelt at length on the social world, it was because he felt that it provided the key to the understanding of character. In his earliest phase as a writer, he was therefore a positivist who faithfully abided by the determinist principle. The responses of his personages are almost automatic: they always reflect in action and in thought the inescapable influences of their background and milieu. But in this first phase of Jaloux's career we can already detect a groping toward new forms. The novelist begins to abandon the static and photographic description of character, in favor of a search for the individual's true self.

Jaloux was thus gradually moving toward a new conception of the novel. He began to question the validity of the naturalistic theories that he had practiced during the first phase of his career. As his horizon widened, and as his insight into human nature deepened, he was drawn almost exclusively to the inner man. In his second period — the period of introspection (1906-1909) — outward reality has ceased to be the fundamental purview of his vision. In creating his personages, Jaloux emphasized only such traits as would suggest man's true physiognomy. But unlike the concrete vision of *Les Sangsues* and *L'Ecole des mariages* in which appearances invariably reveal character, visible reality in the novels of the individual often conceals the truth. Character is no longer the immutable entity that it was in Jaloux's period of naturalism. For the novelist has become keenly aware of man's evolution in the course of time, and he illustrates life's movement by showing his personages enmeshed in a multiplicity of relationships. As he strives to describe the inner person, the author begins to experiment, moreover, with new methods that anticipate his period of poetic imagination. He sometimes relies on intuition, rather than on external evidence, in order to relate his increasingly complex view of reality and of man.

Although Jaloux often resorted to premonitions and insight during his period of introspection, the works which he then produced nevertheless reflect the social preoccupations of the later nineteenth century naturalism. Jaloux, therefore, searched for a new approach to the novel. He strove to achieve an integral way of transcribing life. For he wanted above all to capture the immediacy of human experience. It was that quest to reconstruct a heartfelt reality which made Jaloux so conscious of the paramount importance of the subjective element in man's experience. To portray the reaction of his personages as they confront society and their own self had now become his most immediate concern. The symbolist poets of the late nineteenth century had shown the way of resurrecting prior experience through the synesthetic mingling of sense impressions. Moreover, by using language so as to bring out the evocative or musical power of words, these poets succeeded in conveying almost inexpressible shades of feeling and in recapturing the original freshness of past sensations.

Just prior to the First World War, Jaloux somewhat belatedly introduced into his novels the metaphorical language that he had earlier admired as a devotee of symbolism. This new technique enabled him to translate the totality of human experience and to trace the imperceptible changes that occur in an individual over the span of a great many years. In *Fumées dans la campagne*, a novel of that period, he recaptures the atmosphere of his youth through the device of a narrator. The latter evokes past existence by means of sensory perceptions which miraculously bring back to life people and places as he saw them in the ardor and glow of his adolescent years. This method adds another dimension to Jaloux's work by showing the complexity and disarray of real life as well as the Bergsonian concept of subjective time. In *La Fin d'un beau jour*, one of the novels of his period of poetic imagination, Jaloux's vision turns further inward, as his attention is focussed mainly on representing the fleeting images that flash through the mind of his characters. In this work, the author's poetical vision, that was nourished by the symbolists' feeling for the mystery of man's life, led him into a thorough exploration of the human psyche.

The novelist was thus searching for a style and technique that would most faithfully express the inner reality of the self. In the early 1920's Jaloux came under the influence of Freud. The French author's growing interest in the irrational coincided with the new concern of psychology with the world of dreams. Jaloux's novels of the postwar period reflect the triumph of the psychoanalytic theories. Moreover, his discovery during these years of Gérard de Nerval and the early German romantic writers reinforced his belief that dreams, coincidences and premonitions can serve to bring into the realm of consciousness the repressed feelings of the subconscious.

Although Jaloux continued in *Les Profondeurs de la mer* to rely on sense impressions in order to convey the emotive life of his characters, he no longer attempted to describe it in an orderly way. Rather, he sought to communicate the essence of the human consciousness by describing the flow of images, sensations and recollections which traverse the mind of man. In his attempt to reproduce inner reality as it is actually experienced, he ignored time sequences, by juxtaposing past, present and future. Jaloux's resolve to

151

grant his characters complete freedom of self-analysis ultimately leads to the fragmentation of the personality, as can be seen with Claude Lothaire, the protagonist of *Les Profondeurs de la mer*. However, by the later 1920's, Jaloux became aware that an excessive introspection threatened to pulverize the novel. He thus reunified the fragmented materials of his art and achieves a oneness in *Soleils disparus*, the most characteristic novel of that period, by fusing the dreamlike and the everyday experiences of his personages.

In the next phase of Edmond Jaloux's career — his period of myth and symbol (1932-1940) — he continued to portray the subconscious life of his characters. But the novelist was no longer concerned with analyzing the processes of the mind. He strove to crystallize these states into their corresponding poetic components. For his interest was then drawn mainly toward the universal aspects of the human condition, regardless of place or time. Jaloux's preoccupation with man's fate accounts for his interest in the myths of classical antiquity. By reinterpreting these ancient legends, he might illuminate aspects of human destiny, and arrive at individual, as well as universal truths. If Jaloux now thought in terms of myth, it was because he had acquired the certainty at this time that men were constantly reenacting the fundamental passions inherent to the human race.

In the last phase of his career, which spanned the 1940's Edmond Jaloux moved from the human and terrestrial aspects of life to a cosmic and supernatural vision of existence. He conveys the presence of an invisible and timeless reality in such novels as *Le Culte secret* and *Le Pays des fantômes*. In these works the author emphasizes the mystical experience. His characters gradually lose their concrete identity and are transmuted into spirits that hover between the world of the living and the world of the dead. Likewise, the setting no longer represents a specific geographical location. It has become an imaginary scenery, which suggests an Elysian, translucent and undying world.

For in this period Jaloux projected in his novels his own quest for a transcendental reality, of which the everyday world was but the insubstantial shadow.

Jaloux's protracted development as a novelist is significant not only because it contradicts the notion of dilettantism which his critics attached to him, but also because it reflects the evolution of the writers who are often referred to as "la Génération de 1900." Aside from the anachronistic nature of Jaloux's early *romans de moeurs,* due to his isolation in Marseilles, his subsequent development towards a more lyrical and subjective vision of the world is closely akin to the poetical spirit of such writers as Alain-Fournier, Jean Giraudoux and especially Proust. Moreover, Jaloux's growing preoccupation with his characters' psyche and his attempt to represent its fragmented experience through the inner monologue, reflects also the essential inwardness of such modern writers as Joyce and Virginia Woolf. In his last novels, as we saw, Jaloux evokes a supernatural world where spirits glide freely, liberated from the chains of time and mortality. With its mystical vision of harmony, this final period brings out the meaning of the novelist's credo: art is the only refuge from the miseries of the human fate. Devoted as ever to the esthetic ideals of his youth and to the life of meditation, Jaloux ended by feeling like a stranger in the contemporary world.

BIBLIOGRAPHY

A. WORKS OF EDMOND JALOUX

I. Poetry

Une Ame d'automne. Marseilles: Librairie Flammarion et Aubertin, 1896.

II. Novels

L'Agonie de l'amour. Paris: Mercure de France, 1899.
Les Sangsues. Paris: Société du Mercure de France, 1904, republished by Plon.
Le Jeune homme au masque. Paris: Mercure de France, 1905, republished by Plon.
L'Ecole des mariages. Paris: Société du Mercure de France, 1906, republished by Plon.
Le Démon de la vie. Paris: Librairie Stock, 1908, republished by Plon and Ferenczi.
Le Reste est silence. Paris: Librairie Stock, 1909, republished by Plon.
Les Amours perdues. Paris: Librarie Stock, 1910, republished by Plon.
L'Eventail de crêpe. Paris: Pierre Laffitte, 1911, republished by Plon.
L'Incertaine. Paris: Albin Michel, 1918.
Fumées dans la campagne. Paris: La Renaissance du livre, 1918, republished by Plon.
Au-dessus de la ville. Paris: La Renaissance du Livre, 1920, republished by Plon.
La Fin d'un beau jour. Paris: La Renaissance du Livre, 1921, republished by Plon.

L'Escalier d'or. Paris: La Renaissance du Livre, 1922, republished by Plon.

Les Profondeurs de la mer. Paris: Plon, 1922.

L'Amour de Cécile Fougères. Paris: Ferenczi, 1922.

La Fête nocturne. Paris: Ferenczi, 1922.

Le Rayon dans le brouillard. Paris: Le Divan, 1924.

Le Coin du Cyprès. Paris: La Nouvelle Revue Critique, 1925.

L'Alcyone. Paris: Plon, 1925.

L'ami des jeunes filles. Paris: Ferenczi, 1926.

O Toi que j'eusse aimée! Paris: Plon, 1926.

L'Age d'Or. Paris: Rasmussen, 1926, republished by Ferenczi.

Soleils disparus. Paris: Plon, 1927.

Laetitia. Paris: Plon, 1929.

Sous les Oliviers de Bohème. Paris: Ferenczi, 1932.

La Balance faussée. Paris: Librairie Plon, 1932.

La Grenade mordue. Paris: Librairie Plon, 1933.

Le Dernier jour de la création. Paris: Librairie Plon, 1935.

Le Voyageur. Paris: Librairie Plon, 1935.

La Chute d'Icare. Paris: La Palatine, à la Librairie Plon, 1936.

L'Egarée. Paris: Librairie Plon, 1936.

L'Oiseau-Lyre. Paris: Arthème Fayard, 1938.

La Capricieuse. Paris: Plon, 1939.

Le Miroir de Vénus. Paris: Arthème Fayard, 1939 – (Les Oeuvres Libres).

Les Visiteurs. Paris: Plon, 1940.

Le Vent souffle sur la flamme. Fribourg: Egloff L.U.F., 1941.

Le Pouvoir des choses. Geneva: Edition du Milieu du Monde, 1941.

La comédie féminine. Paris-Lausanne: L'Echiquier, 1946.

La Maison des rêves. Vevey: La Table Ronde, 1947.

Le Culte secret. Paris: La Table Ronde, 1947.

Le Pays des fantômes. Lyons: Imprimerie Artistique en Couleurs, 1948.

La Constellation. Geneva: Edition du Milieu du Monde, 1950.

Le Dernier Acte. Paris: Plon, 1950.

III. Short Stories

"La Nuit d'angoisse," *L'Hermitage*, I (1905), pp. 220-230.
"Protée," *L'Hermitage*, I (1906), pp. 281-290.
Le Boudoir de Proserpine. Paris: Dorbon, 1910.
La Branche morte. Paris: Plon, 1928.
Les Routes du bel univers. Paris: Librairie Plon, 1936.

IV. Essays and Critical Works

L'Esprit des Livres (Première série). Paris: Librairie Plon, 1923.
Figures étrangères. (Première série). Paris: Librarie Plon-Nourrit, 1925.
Marseille. Portrait de la France. Paris: Edition Emile Paul 1926.
De Pascal à Barrès. "L'esprit des livres" (Deuxième série). Paris: Librairie Plon, 1927.
Rainer Maria Rilke. Paris: Edition Emile Paul, 1927.
De Pascal à Barrès. "L'esprit des livres" (Cinquième série). Paris: Librairie Plon, 1931.
Perspectives et Personnages. "L'esprit des livres" (Troisième série). Paris: Librairie Plon, 1931.
Au Pays du roman. Paris: Editions R.-A. Corrêa, 1931.
Du Rêve à la réalité. Paris: Editions R.-A. Corrêa, 1932.
Discours de réception à l'Académie française. Paris: Librairie Plon, 1937.
Souvenirs sur Henri de Régnier. Lausanne: Librairie F. Rouge et Co. S. A., 1941.
Edgar Poe et les femmes. Geneva: Editions du Milieu du Monde, 1942.
Les Saisons littéraires 1896-1903. Fribourg: Editions de l'Université de Fribourg, 1942.
D'Eschyle à Giraudoux. Fribourg: Egloff, L. U. F., 1946.
Introduction à l'histoire de la littérature française, I des ori-

gines à la fin du moyen age. Geneva: Editions Pierre Cailler, 1946.

Introduction à l'histoire de la littérature française, II le XVIe siècle. Geneva: Editions Pierre Cailler, 1947.

Goethe: l'homme et son oeuvre. Paris: Librairie Arthème Fayard, 1949.

Les Saisons littéraires 1904-1914. Paris: Librairie Plon, 1950.

Essences, édition revue et augmentée. Paris: Librairie Plon, 1952.

Visages Français. Paris: Editions Albin Michel, 1954.

V. Articles in Books and Periodicals [1]

"L'Oeuvre de Marcel Proust," *Les Ecrits Nouveaux*, I - II (1920), pp. 101-107.

"La découverte de l'enfant," *La Revue Universelle*, I (April-June, 1920), pp. 223-227.

"Jean Giraudoux," *La Revue Européenne*, I (March 1, 1923), pp. 37-47.

"Observations sur la psychanalyse," *Le Disque Vert*, numéro spécial (1924), pp. 28-37.

"Dialogue sur Rainer Maria Rilke," *La Revue Générale*, II (1929), pp. 20-26.

"Henry James et 'Un portrait de femme'," *La Revue Hebdomadaire*, (December, 1933).

"Le roman et l'actualité," *Chroniques*, (June 28, 1939).

"Le Maréchal Pétain," *Le Mois Suisse*, XLIII (1942).

"Francis de Miomandre, conteur féerique," in *D'Eschyle à Giraudoux*. Fribourg: Egloff, L. U. F., 1946, pp. 237-249.

"Actualité de la tragédie grecque," in *D'Eschyle à Giraudoux*.

"Mort de Virginia Woolf," in *D'Eschyle à Giraudoux*, pp. 253-259.

"La solitude morale dans la littérature romande," in *D'Eschyle à Giraudoux*, pp. 137-157.

"Après la guerre de 1919 . . . ," in *Hommage à Maurice Betz*. Paris: Editions Emile-Paul Frères, 1949, pp. 71-84.

VI. Contributions to Other Volumes

Prefaces

Tieck, Louis. *La Coupe d'or et autres contes.* Paris. Denoël et Steele, n. d.

Le Cinquantenaire du Symbolisme. Paris: Editions des Bibliothèques Nationales, 1936.

Huxley, Aldous. *Deux ou trois grâces.* Paris: Librairie Stock, 1931.

Milosz, Oscar Vladislas. *Oeuvres complètes.* I *Poèmes.* Fribourg: Egloff, 1944.

La Dernière amitié de Rainer Maria Rilke, lettres inédites à Madame Eloui Bey. Paris: Robert Laffont, 1949.

Mauriac, François. *Le Romancier et ses personnages.* Paris: Corrêa, 1952.

Avec Marcel Proust, suivi de dix-sept lettres inédites de Proust. Paris-Geneva: La Palatine, 1953.

Lautréamont. *Oeuvres complètes.* Les Chants de Maldoror. Poésies. Lettres. Paris: José Corti, 1961.

VII. Translations of Jaloux's Works

Humos en el campo, por Edmundo Jaloux. Prólogo de Vicente Blasco-Ibáñez, Versión española de José Luengo. Valencia: Prometeo, n. d.

Die Tiefen des Meeres, von Edmond Jaloux. Berechtigte Ubertragung aus dem Französischen von N. Collin, mit einem Vorwort von Thomas Mann. Volksverband der Bücherfreunde, Wegweiser Verlag, G. m. b., Berlin: 1928.

B. WORKS OF OTHER AUTHORS

I. Books

Balakian, Anna. *The Symbolist Movement: A Critical Appraisal.* New York: Random House, 1967.

Béguin, Albert. *L'Ame romantique et le rêve:* essai sur le

romantisme allemand et la poésie française. Marseilles: Editions des Cahiers du Sud, 1937.

Bertaut, Jules. *Le Roman nouveau.* Paris: La Renaissance du livre, 1921.

Booth, Wayne C. *The Rhetoric of Fiction.* Chicago & London: The University of Chicago Press, 1963.

Bowen, Ray Preston. *The Novels of Ferdinand Fabre.* Boston: Richard G. Badger, The Gorham Press, 1918.

Bowra, C. M. *The Greek Experience.* London: Richard Clay and Company, Ltd., Weidenfeld and Nicolson, 1957.

Brogan, Denis William. *The Development of Modern France 1870-1939.* New and revised ed.; London: H. Hamilton, 1967.

Delétang-Tardif, Yanette. *Edmond Jaloux.* Paris: La Table Ronde, 1947.

Du Bos, Charles. *Approximations.* Paris: Fayard, 1965.

Dumesnil, René. *Le Réalisme et le Naturalisme,* ed. J. Calvet. Paris: del Duca de Gigord, 1955.

Erckman, Emile et Chatrian, Alexandre. *Contes et romans populaires.* Paris: J. Hetzel Editeur, 1867.

Estaunié, Edouard. *Roman et Province.* Marseilles: Robert Laffont, 1943.

Etiemble, René. *Littérature Dégagée 1942-1953.* Paris: Librairie Gallimard, 1955.

Gide, André. *Découvrons Henri Michaux.* Paris: Gallimard, 1941.

——. *Journal 1889-1939.* Paris: Librairie Gallimard, 1941.

Goodrich, Norma Lorre. *Myths of the Hero.* New York: The Orion Press, 1962.

Graves, Robert. *The Greek Myths.* 2 vols. Baltimore, Maryland: Penguin Books, 1955.

Hamsun, Knut, pseud. of Knut Pedersen. *Der Wanderer: Romantrilogie.* Munich: Albert Langen - Georg Müller Verlag, G. m. b., 1932.

Hellens, Franz, pseud. of Frédéric van Ermengem. *Nouvelles Réalités fantastiques.* Paris - Brussels, Les Ecrits, 1941.

Hesnard, A. *L'Oeuvre de Freud et son importance pour le*

monde moderne. Préface de Maurice Merleau-Ponty.
Paris: Payot, 1960.

Huysmans, J.-K., *A Rebours*. Avec une préface de l'auteur
écrite vingt ans après. Paris: Editions Fasquelle, 1968.

Ibsen, Henrik. *When We Dead Awaken*. Newly translated
from the Norwegian by Michael Meyer. London: Rupert
Hart-Davis. Soho Square, 1960.

Jaeger, Werner. *Paideia: the Ideals of Greek Culture*. Vol. I:
Archaic Greece, the Mind of Athens. 2nd ed., trans. Gilbert
Highet. New York: Oxford University Press, 1945.

James, Henry. *Stories of Writers and Artists*, edited with an
introduction by F. O. Matthiesen. New York: New Direc-
tions, 1944.

James, William. *The Varieties of Religious Experience*. New
York: Longmans, Green, and Co., 1925.

Kolbert, Jack. *Edmond Jaloux et sa critique littéraire*. Pré-
cédé d'une préface d'André Maurois. Geneva: Librairie
Droz, Paris: Minard, 1962.

Lacher, Walter. *Le Réalisme dans le roman contemporain*:
essai sur quelques romanciers français d'aujourd'hui.
Geneva: Imprimerie Centrale, 1940.

Le Blond, Maurice. *Essai sur le Naturisme*. Paris: Edition du
Mercure de France, 1896.

Lemaitre, Georges. *From Cubism to Surrealism in French
Literature*. London: Oxford University Press, Cambridge,
Mass., Harvard University Press, 1941.

Martin du Gard, Maurice. *Les Mémorables 1918-1923*. Paris:
Flammarion, 1957.

———. *Les Mémorables 1924-1930*. Paris: Flammarion, 1960.

Masur, Gerhard. *Prophets of Yesterday*: Studies in European
Culture 1890-1914. New York: The Macmillan Company,
1961.

Michaud, Guy. *Message poétique du Symbolisme*. Tome I:
L'Aventure poétique. Tome II: La Révolution poétique.
Tome III: L'Univers poétique. Paris: Librairie Nizet, 1951,
1954, 1955.

Michaux, Henri. *Voyage en Grande Garabagne*. Collection

"Métamorphoses". Paris: Editions de la N.R.F., 1936.

Miomandre, Francis de. *Le Pavillon du Mandarin*. Paris: Emile Paul, 1921.

——. *Mallarmé*. Paris: Bader-Dufour, 1948.

Mornet, Daniel. *Introduction à l'étude des écrivains français d'aujourd'hui*. Paris: Boivin et Co., 1939.

Morrow, Christine. *Le Roman irréaliste dans les littératures contemporaines de langues française et anglaise*. Toulouse: Imprimerie Toulousaine Lion Raoul, 1941.

Newman, Pauline. *Un Romancier périgordin: Eugène Le Roy et son temps*. Paris: Nouvelles Editions Latines, 1957.

Nilsson, Martin P. *A History of Greek Religion*. Trans. F. J. Fielden. Oxford: The Clarendon Press, 1925.

Peyre, Henri. *Shelley et la France:* Lyrisme anglais et lyrisme français au dix-neuvième siècle. Cairo: Imprimerie Paul Barbey, 1935.

Poulet, Georges. *Etudes sur le temps humain*. Tome II: La distance intérieure. Paris: Plon, 1952.

Proust, Marcel. *A la Recherche du temps perdu*. Tome XIV: Le Temps retrouvé (1). Tome XV: Le Temps retrouvé (2). Paris: Gallimard, 1927.

Raimond, Michel. *La Crise du roman des lendemains du Naturalisme aux années vingt*. Paris: Librairie José Corti, 1966.

Raynaud, Ernest. *En marge de la mêlée symboliste*. Paris: Mercure de France, 1936.

Ricord, Maurice. *Marseille, cité littéraire*. Marseilles: Robert Laffont, 1941.

Rilke, Rainer Maria. *Gedichte*. Dritter Teil, Neue Gedichte — Duineser Elegien, Die Sonette an Orpheus — Letzte Gedichte und Fragmentarishes. Leipzig: Insel-Verlag, 1927.

Segalen, Victor. *Lettres de Chine*. (adressées à Claudel, Huvsmans, Jaloux, Rimbaud) Présentées par Jean-Louis Bédouin. Paris: Plon, 1967.

Seignobos, Charles. *Histoire sincère de la nation française;*

essai d'une histoire de l'évolution du peuple français. Paris: Editions Rieder, 1945.

Soltau, Roger H. *French Parties and Politics.* London: Oxford University Press, 1922.

Vaudoyer, Jean-Louis. *Discours prononcés dans la séance publique tenue par l'Académie française.* Paris: Firmin-Didot, 1950.

II. Articles in Books and Periodicals

Assailly, Gisèle d'. "Rencontre avec Edmond Jaloux," *La Gazette des Lettres,* (May 17, 1947).

Beaunier, André. "Les Romans d'Edmond Jaloux," *Revue des Deux Mondes,* LVII (June 1, 1920), pp. 697-708.

Betz, Maurice. "Edmond Jaloux," *Bibliothèque Universelle et Revue de Genève,* II (August, 1926), pp. 188-199.

Bidou, Henri. "Parmi les livres: La Fin d'un beau jour," *Revue de Paris,* (March 15, 1921), pp. 382-384.

Billy, André. "Soleils disparus," *L'Oeuvre,* (August 9, 1927).

——. "Les Souvenirs d'Edmond Jaloux," *Le Figaro Littéraire,* (November 15, 1950).

Brion. Marcel. "Edmond Jaloux," *Cahiers du Sud,* LIV, No. 370 (February-March, 1963), pp. 456-458.

Chenevière, Jacques. "Hommage à Edmond Jaloux," *Vie, Art, Cité* (No. 6, 1949), pp. 24-26.

——. "Un sourcier, un sage," in *Retours et images.* Lausanne, Edition Rencontre, 1966.

Crémieux, Benjamin. "Edmond Jaloux," *La Nouvelle Revue Française, dixième année* (January-June, 1923), pp. 597-611.

Daniel-Rops. "Histoire de la littérature française par Edmond Jaloux," *Carrefour,* III (March 8, 1947).

Daudet, Léon. "L'Egarée," *Candide,* (March 17, 1938).

Debrix, Jean. "Les Livres: Quand Jaloux se critique lui-même," *Liberté,* (April, 1933).

Delétang-Tardif, Yanette. "Edmond Jaloux: Le regard intérieur," *Revue Politique et Littéraire, Revue Bleue,* (1936), pp. 657-659.

——. "Edmond Jaloux, romancier," *Psyché, quatrième année,*
No. 33 (July, 1949), pp. 665-667.

Du Bos, Charles. "Les Profondeurs de la mer," *La Nouvelle*
Revue Française, (February 1, 1923), pp. 448-455.

Duhamel, Georges. *Allocution à l'occasion de la mort de*
M. Edmond Jaloux: Séance du premier septembre 1949.
Paris: Firmin-Didot, 1949.

Elcombe, Marie Louisa Crapoulet. "Edmond Jaloux — His
Beginnings as a Regionalist," *The French Review,* XLIII,
No. 4 (March, 1970), pp. 580-587.

Finot, Louis-Jean. "Soleils disparus," *La Revue,* (September 1, 1927).

Fosca, François. "Edmond Jaloux et les littératures étrangères," *La Revue Hebdomadaire,* III (March-April, 1926),
pp. 493-500.

Frye, Northrop. "The Archetypes of Literature," in *Myth*
and Literature: Contemporary Theory and Practice, ed.,
John B. Vickery; Lincoln: University of Nebraska Press,
1966.

Gérard-Gailly, E. "Edmond Jaloux," *Revue du Temps Pré-*
sent, II (July, 1912), p. 420.

Germain, André. "Soleils disparus," *La Revue Européenne*
(October 1927), pp. 380-382.

Hellens, Franz, pseud. of Frédéric van Ermengem. "Soleils
disparus," *Rouge et Noir,* (October-November, 1927).

Henriot, Emile. "Trois prix littéraires et trois romanciers:
Tharaud, Jaloux, Boulanger," *La Vie des Peuples,* I (1920),
pp. 395-404.

——. "Près de Lausanne: Edmond Jaloux est mort," *Le*
Monde (August 24, 1949).

——. "Hommage à Edmond Jaloux," *Vie, Art, Cité* (No. 6,
1949), pp. 18-19.

Kanters, Robert. "Edmond Jaloux ou une critique d'interces-
seur," *La Table Ronde,* LIII (May, 1952), pp. 131-133.

Kemp, Robert. "Edmond Jaloux le rêveur," *Les Nouvelles*
Littéraires, No. 1069 (February 26, 1948).

Kolbert, Jack. "Edmond Jaloux: literary critic," *Kentucky*

Foreign Language Quarterly, IV (1957), pp. 74-82.

——. "Edmond Jaloux and his Contemporaries," *The French Review,* XXXI, No. 4 (February, 1958), pp. 283-291.

——. "Edmond Jaloux as a popularizer of English literature," *The French Review,* XXXIV, No. 5 (April, 1961), pp. 432-439.

Lacretelle, Jacques de. "Hommage à Edmond Jaloux," *Vie, Art, Cité* (No. 6, 1949).

Lebois, André. "Transfiguration du réel dans nos lettres d'aujourd'hui," *Littératures V,* Annales publiées par la Faculté des Lettres de Toulouse, année VI (February, 1957), pp. 21-45.

Martin du Gard, Maurice. "Opinions et portraits: Edmond Jaloux," *Les Nouvelles Littéraires,* LIV (October 27, 1923).

——. "Edmond Jaloux," *L'Epoque,* (August 26, 1949).

Maubert, Alfred. "Au bord du lac," *Les Nouvelles Littéraires,* No. 1668 (August 20, 1959).

Mauclair, Camille. "Les Sangsues," *La Revue Universelle,* (1904), p. 510.

Mauriac, François. "Un homme de lettres: Edmond Jaloux," *Le Figaro,* (August 29, 1949).

Maurois, André. "Edmond Jaloux ou l'instinct de l'éternel," *Les Nouvelles Littéraires,* quarantième année, No. 1815 (June 14, 1962).

Miomandre, Francis de. "Les Profondeurs de la mer," *Les Nouvelles Littéraires,* (October 28, 1922).

——. "Avec Edmond Jaloux dans la rue des Tonneliers," *Les Nouvelles Littéraires,* No. 741 (December 26, 1936).

——. "Prime Jeunesse," *France-Asie,* V (August-December, 1949), pp. 383-386.

——. "Edmond Jaloux," in *Books Abroad,* University of Oklahoma Press, (January, 1950).

Mondor, Henri. "Portrait d'un humaniste," *Les Nouvelles Littéraires,* No. 1376 (January 14, 1954).

Place, Joseph. "Les Profondeurs de la mer," *Chronique des Lettres Françaises,* I (1923), pp. 118-119.

Praviel, Armand. "Un Marseillais pessimiste: Edmond Jaloux," *Le Correspondant,* CCXCV (April-June, 1924).

Rachilde. "Les Sangsues," *Mercure de France,* L (May, 1904), pp. 462-463.

——. "L'Ecole des mariages," *Mercure de France,* LXV (February 15, 1907), pp. 691-692.

Reed, Verner. "The Soul of Paris," *The Atlantic Monthly,* XCVIII (July, 1906), pp. 336-342.

Régnier, Henri de. "La Grenade mordue," *Le Figaro,* (December 28, 1933).

Souday, Paul. "Fumées dans la campagne," *Le Temps,* (August 1, 1918).

Thibaudet, Albert. "Réflexions sur la littérature: romans pendant la guerre," *La Nouvelle Revue Française,* sixième année (June 1, 1919), pp. 129-142.

Traz, Robert de. "Chroniques, Les Livres: L'Egarée par Edmond Jaloux," *Revue Hebdomadaire,* (March 26, 1938), pp. 484-487.

Verdurin. "Edmond Jaloux et le courage," *L'Epoque,* (August 24, 1949).

Whiteing, Richard. "Artistic Paris," *The Century Magazine,* XXXVIII (May-October, 1900), pp. 400-414.

Winkler, André. "Crónica de Suiza: Edmond Jaloux," *Insula* Madrid, año IV, No. 47 (November 15, 1949), p. 2.

C. UNPUBLISHED MATERIAL

Autograph letter from Edmond Jaloux to André Gide, May 26, 1897, 945-1 (Paris: Bibliothèque littéraire Jacques Doucet).

Autograph letter from Edmond Jaloux to André Gide, August 1, 1902, 945-2 (Paris: Bibliothèque littéraire Jacques Doucet).

Autograph letter from Edmond Jaloux to André Gide, September 22, 1902, 945-3 (Paris: Bibliothèque littéraire Jacques Doucet).

Letter from Paul Claudel to Edmond Jaloux, Tokyo, December, 6, 1921. (Typewritten copy given by Madame Edmond Jaloux).

Letter from Henri Bergson to Edmond Jaloux, Paris, April 14, 1938. (Typewritten copy transmitted by Madame Edmond Jaloux).

D. OTHER SOURCES

Personal interview with the late Jean-Louis Vaudoyer, art critic. Paris, December 15, 1959.

Personal interview with Madame Edmond Jaloux. Lausanne, Switzerland, December 23, 1959.

Personal interview with the late Emile Henriot, novelist and literary critic. Paris, January 25, 1960.

Personal interview with the late Madame Charles Du Bos, Paris, June 27, 1960.

Personal interviews with Gabriel Marcel. Paris, December 2, 1960; June 19 and June 23, 1971.

Personal interviews with Madame Yanette Delétang-Tardif. Paris: January 22, 1960; June 13, 1961.

NOTES TO INTRODUCTION

1. Yanette Delétang-Tardif, *Edmond Jaloux* (Paris: La Table Ronde, 1947), pp. 51-59.

2. André Winkler, "Crónica de Suiza: Edmond Jaloux," *Insula*, Madrid, año IV, No. XLVII, (November 15, 1949), p. 2.

3. Emile Henriot, "Trois prix littéraires et trois romanciers: Tharaud, Jaloux, Boulanger," *La Vie des Peuples*, I (1920), p. 395; E. Gérard-Gailly, "Edmond Jaloux," *Revue du Temps Présent*, II (July, 1912), p. 420; Daniel-Rops, "Histoire de la littérature française par Edmond Jaloux," *Carrefour*, III (March 8, 1947).

4. Autograph letters from Edmond Jaloux to André Gide, August 1, 1902, 945-2; Edmond Jaloux to André Gide, September 22, 1902, 945-3 (Paris: Bibliothèque littéraire Jacques Doucet).

5. In both novels the main characters crave absolute freedom; in both cases they discover that the sinner comes closer to an understanding of life than the just man.

6. François Mauriac, "Un homme de lettres: Edmond Jaloux," *Le Figaro*, (August 29, 1949); Georges Duhamel, *Allocution à l'occasion de la mort de M. Edmond Jaloux*: Séance du premier septembre 1949 (Paris: Firmin-Didot, 1949), p. 4.

7. Henriot, *loc. cit.*, p. 399; Maurice Martin du Gard, "Opinions et portraits: Edmond Jaloux," *Les Nouvelles Littéraires*, LIV (October 27, 1923).

8. *Cinquantenaire du Symbolisme*, préface par Edmond Jaloux, (Paris: Editions des Bibliothèques Nationales, 1936), pp. vi-vii, xiv-xv.

NOTES TO CHAPTER I

1. Yanette Delétang-Tardif, *Edmond Jaloux* (Paris: La Table Ronde, 1947), pp. 51-53.

2. Maurice Martin du Gard, "Edmond Jaloux," *L'Epoque* (August 26, 1949).

3. Edmond Jaloux, *Marseille: Portrait de la France* (Paris: Edition Emile Paul, 1926), *passim*.

4. Jaloux was then 13 years old and already an avid reader of travel books and stories of adventure; see his chapter "La fin de l'enfance" (*Les saisons littéraires 1896-1903* [Fribourg: Editions de l'Université, 1942]), p. 14.

5. Michel Raimond takes important notice of this in *La Crise du roman Des lendemains du Naturalisme aux années vingt* (Paris: Librairie José Corti, 1966), pp. 25-43, and offers a searching analysis of the movement's impending disintegration.

6. *Les Saisons littéraires 1896-1903*, p. 87.

7. Edmond Jaloux, *Les Saisons littéraires: 1904-1914* (Paris: Librairie Plon, 1950), pp. 104-108.

8. Edmond Jaloux, *Avec Marcel Proust*, suivi de dix-sept lettres inédites de Proust, (Paris, Geneva: La Palatine, 1953), pp. 14-15.

9. Jaloux's obsession with the theme of cruelty appears throughout his work. *Les Sangsues* (1904) and *Le Miroir de Vénus* (1939) for example describe a group of adolescents mercilessly victimizing their prey.

10. *Les Saisons littéraires 1904-1914*, p. 35.

11. Jean-Louis Vaudoyer, *Discours prononcés à l'Académie française* (Paris: Firmin Didot, 1950), p. 8.

12. *Les Saisons littéraires 1896-1903*, pp. 28-29.

13. *Ibid.*, p. 25.

14. Francis de Miomandre, "Avec Edmond Jaloux dans la rue des Tonneliers," *Les Nouvelles Littéraires*, No. 741 (December 26, 1936), p. 3.

15. *Les Saisons littéraires*, II, pp. 108-112.

16. *Les Saisons littéraires*, I, p. 161.

17. Jack Kolbert, "Edmond Jaloux and his Contemporaries," *The French Review*, XXXI, No. 4 (February, 1958), p. 284.

18. Autograph letter from Edmond Jaloux to André Gide, September 22, 1902, 945-3 (Paris: Bibliothèque littéraire Jacques Doucet).

19. Francis de Miomandre, *Mallarmé* (Paris: Bader-Dufour, 1948), pp. 25, 34.

20. Henri Peyre, *Shelley et la France*: lyrisme anglais et lyrisme français au dix-neuvième siècle (Cairo: Imprimerie Paul Berbey, 1935), p. 420.

21. *Les Saisons littéraires*, I, p. 50.

22. Francis de Miomandre, "Prime jeunesse," *France-Asie*, V (August-December, 1949), p. 384.

23. Gide was turning away from the overrefined language of such decadent poets as Pierre Louys and Marcel Schwob since the mid-nineties.

24. Autograph letter from Edmond Jaloux to André Gide, May 25, 1897, 945-1 (Paris: Bibliothèque littéraire Jacques Doucet).

25. Miomandre, "Avec Edmond Jaloux dans la rue des Tonneliers," p. 3.

26. Maurice Le Blond, *Essai sur le Naturisme* (Paris: Edition du Mercure de France, 1896), pp. 113-127.

27. Guy Michaud, *Message Poétique du Symbolisme: L'Univers poétique* (3 vols.; Paris: Librairie Nizet, 1955), III, pp. 527-528.

28. *Ibid.*, p. 531.

29. *Les Saisons littéraires*, I, p. 133.

30. Jack Kolbert, *Edmond Jaloux et sa critique littéraire* (Geneva: Librairie Droz, 1962), p. 19.

31. Edmond Jaloux, *Souvenirs sur Henri de Régnier* (Lausanne: Librairie F. Rouge & Co., 1941), p. 20.

32. *Les Saisons littéraires, I*, pp. 279-287.

33. Knowing Jaloux's natural exuberance, Gide advocated a greater economy of expression. "Pourquoi ne pas écrire un roman réaliste?" he is supposed to have suggested to his southern friend. Quoted by Mme Edmond Jaloux during a personal interview with her, Lausanne, December 23, 1959.

34. Autograph letter from Edmond Jaloux to André Gide, August 1, 1902, 945-2 (Paris: Bibliothèque littéraire Jacques Doucet).

35. This relation of pupil to teacher characterizes the tone of Jaloux's early correspondence with Gide.

36. *Les Saisons littéraires*, I, p. 283.

NOTES TO CHAPTER II

1. Edmond Jaloux, *Les Saisons littéraires: 1904-1914* (Paris: Librairie Plon, 1950), pp. 66-71, 91, 108.

2. Frequented not only by poets, but also by men in the world of politics and letters, the cafés of the left bank effected a rapprochement between artistic bohemia and the bourgeoisie which made them more congenial for Jaloux than the radical cabarets of Montmartre.

3. *Les Saisons littéraires 1904-1914*, p. 46.

4. *Ibid.*, pp. 14, 52-64, 127-132.

5. J.-L. Vaudoyer (1883-1961): a sensitive art critic and essayist who also wrote evocative novels such as *Les Permissions de Clément Bellin* and *La Bien-Aimée*.

6. Auguste Gilbert de Voisins (1877-1939). Like Jaloux, this novelist went through a literary evolution. Thus an early novel *le Bar de la Fourche* (1909) reflects the minute realism of the late XIXth century, while such later works as *Ecrit en Chine* (1913) and *L'Absence et le retour* (1929) reveal the exotic dream of the poet.

7. *Les Saisons littéraires*, II, p. 210.

8. Richard Whiteing, "Artistic Paris," *The Century Magazine*, XXXVIII (May-October, 1900), pp. 400-414; Verner Reed, "The Soul of Paris," *The Atlantic Monthly*, XCVIII (July, 1906), pp. 336-342.

9. Edmond Jaloux, *Souvenirs sur Henri de Régnier* (Lausanne: Librairie F. Rouge & Co., 1941), pp. 35-37.

10. *Ibid.*, p. 38.

11. Maurice Martin du Gard, *Les Mémorables 1918-1923* (Paris: Flammarion, 1957), pp. 109-113.

12. *Souvenirs sur Henri de Régnier*, pp. 39-40.

13. Jaloux's highly individualistic concept of love and his propensity

for spiritual friendships with women are clearly revealed in his two introductions to his work: *Edgar Poe et les femmes* (Geneva: Editions du Milieu du Monde, 1942).

14. Edmond Jaloux married Germaine Koïré during the war, in Paris, December 1916.

15. In this connection, it is interesting to note that Jaloux knew Marcel Proust. Though he met him only in 1917, he had been corresponding with him since 1903 when he first discovered Proust's subtle mind in *Les Plaisirs et les Jours*. See Jaloux's *Avec Marcel Proust* (Paris: La Palatine, 1953), pp. 14-15.

16. *Les Saisons littéraires*, II, pp. 222-229.

17. Madame Charles Du Bos, who was, during that period, the hostess of a literary salon, stated that Jaloux had met Paul Bourget at her home, around 1910, and that the southern novelist greatly admired the author of *Le Disciple*. Personal interview with Mme Du Bos, Paris, June 27, 1960.

18. Roger Soltau, *French Parties and Politics* (London: Oxford University Press, 1922), pp. 40-52; Charles Seignobos, *The Evolution of the French People*, trans. Catherine Alison Phillips (New York: Alfred A. Knopf, 1938), pp. 365-369.

19. Gerhard Masur, *Prophets of Yesterday: Studies in European Culture 1890-1914* (New York: The Macmillan Company, 1961), pp. 405-410.

20. Georges Lemaitre, *From Cubism to Surrealism in French Literature* (Cambridge: Harvard University Press, 1941), pp. 71-84.

21. Jaloux expressed himself forcefully on this question. "Il est indubitable", he said about 1905, "que le roman subit une crise fondamentale; il lui faut se renouveler ou disparaître." Quoted by Michel Raimond in *La Crise du roman des lendemains du naturalisme aux années vingt* (Paris: Librairie José Corti, 1966), p. 101.

22. Jean-Louis Vaudoyer, *Discours prononcés à l'Académie française: réponse d'Emile Henriot* (Paris: Firmin Didot, 1950), pp. 51-52.

23. *Souvenirs sur Henri de Régnier*, pp. 43-63.

24. Vaudoyer, *Discours . . .*, pp. 18-19.

25. Edmond Jaloux, "Après la guerre de 1919 . . .," in *Hommage à Maurice Betz* (Paris: Paul Frères, 1949) pp. 71-84.

26. Personal interview with M. Gabriel Marcel, Paris, December 2, 1960.

27. Edmond Jaloux, "L'Oeuvre de Marcel Proust," *Les Ecrits Nouveaux* (1920), 1-2, pp. 101-107.

28. Maurice Martin du Gard, "Edmond Jaloux," *L'Epoque*, (August 26, 1949).

29. François Fosca, "Edmond Jaloux et les littératures étrangères," *La Revue Hebdomadaire*, III (March-April, 1926), pp. 493-500.

30. Edmond Jaloux, *Du Rêve à la réalité* (Paris: Editions R. A. Corrêa, 1932), *passim*.

31. Edmond Jaloux, "Dialogue sur Rainer Maria Rilke," *La Revue Générale*, II (1929), pp. 20-26.

32. Edmond Jaloux, "Mrs. Dalloway par Virginia Woolf," in *Au Pays du roman* (Paris: Editions Corrêa, 1931), pp. 185-198.

33. Gisèle d'Assailly, "Rencontre avec Edmond Jaloux," *La Gazette des Lettres* (May 17, 1947).

34. Edmond Jaloux, "Le roman et l'actualité," *Chroniques*, (June 28, 1939).

35. Edmond Jaloux, *Le Cinquantenaire du Symbolisme* (Paris: Bibliothèque Nationale, 1936).

36. *Discours de réception de M. Edmond Jaloux à l'Académie française et réponse de M. Georges Lecomte* (Paris: Librairie Plon, 1937), pp. 3-71.

37. Alfred Maubert, "Au bord du lac," *Les Nouvelles Littéraires*, (August 20, 1959); Edmond Jaloux, "Le Maréchal Pétain," *Le Mois Suisse*, XLIII (1942), pp. 24-29.

38. The feeling of insurmountable solitude that permeates the fiction of French Switzerland is brought out by Jaloux in his essay "La Solitude morale dans la littérature romande," (*D'Eschyle à Giraudoux* [Fribourg: Egloff L.U.F., 1947]); pp. 137-157.

39. André Lebois, "Transfiguration du réel dans nos lettres d'aujourd' hui," *Littératures* V, Annales publiées par la Faculté des Lettres de Toulouse, (February 1957), pp. 40-43.

40. Verdurin, "Edmond Jaloux et le courage," *L'Epoque*, (August 24, 1949).

41. Emile Henriot, "Près de Lausanne: Edmond Jaloux est mort," *Le Monde*, (August 24, 1949).

NOTES TO CHAPTER III

1. Marie Louisa Crapoulet Elcombe brings out with great clarity Jaloux's role as a champion of regional literature during his beginnings as a Southern writer in her article "Edmond Jaloux — His Beginnings as a Regionalist," *The French Review*, XLIII, No. 4 (March, 1970), pp. 580-587.

2. Pauline Newman, *Un Romancier périgordin Eugène Le Roy et son temps* (Paris: Nouvelles Editions Latines, 1957), pp. 31-40.

3. René Dumesnil, *Le Réalisme et le Naturalisme* (Paris: del Duca de Gigord, 1955), p. 156.

4. Ray Preston Bowen, *The Novels of Ferdinand Fabre* (Boston: Richard G. Badger, The Gorham Press, 1918).

5. Erckmann-Chatrian, *Contes et Romans populaires* (Paris: J. Hetzel, Editeur, 1867), *passim*.

5a. Edouard Estaunié, *Roman et Province* (Marseilles: Robert Laffont, 1943), pp. 55-72.

6. Edmond Jaloux, *De pascal à Barrès*, l'esprit des livres troisième série (Paris: Librairie Plon, 1931), p. 171.

7. Edmond Jaloux, *Marseille: Portrait de la France* (Paris: Edition Emile-Paul Frères, 1926), pp. 8-15, 70 ff.

8. "Ses romans," wrote Armand Praviel, "sont une ardente protestation

171

contre la société et son goût du lucre," in "Un Marseillais pessimiste: Edmond Jaloux," *Le Correspondant,* CCXCV (April-June, 1924), pp. 999-1000.

9. Yanette Delétang-Tardif, *Edmond Jaloux* (Paris: La Table Ronde, 1947), p. 24.

10. Edmond Jaloux, *Les Sangsues* (Paris: Société du Mercure de France, 1904), p. 7.

11. *Les Sangsues,* p. 365.

12. Rachilde suggests this fixity by viewing the priest as the eternal victim of a greedy society; see her article "Les Sangsues," *Mercure de France,* L (May, 1904), p. 462.

13. *Les Sangsues,* p. 175.

14. *Ibid.,* pp. 384-385.

15. The contrast between Barbaroux and Mathenot calls to mind two much stranger figures in *Les Faux monnayeurs:* the cynical Strouvilhou and the ingenuous Azaïs.

16. *Les Sangsues,* pp. 9-10.

17. *Ibid.,* p. 362.

18. In his essay on Balzac, Jaloux emphasizes this deliberate enlargement of the personality: ". . . il faut *titaniser* l'homme, l'arracher à sa vie médiocre; lui donner des passions atroces ou sublimes, mais toujours surhumaines"; see his essay on "Balzac" (*Visages français* [Paris: Editions Albin Michel, 1954]), pp. 107-108.

19. *Les Sangsues,* p. 362.

20. *Les Sangsues,* pp. 84-85.

21. Francis de Miomandre, *Le Pavillon du Mandarin* (Paris: Emile Paul, 1921), p. 261.

22. Maurice Ricord, *Marseille, cité littéraire* (Marseilles: Robert Laffont, 1941), p. 264.

23. Miomandre, *op. cit.,* p. 266.

24. Rachilde, "L'Ecole des mariages," *Mercure de France,* LXV (February 15, 1907), p. 691.

25. Edmond Jaloux, *L'Ecole des mariages* (Paris: Société du Mercure de France, 1906), pp. 45-46.

26. *Ibid.,* pp. 64-65.

27. *Ibid.,* p. 65.

28. *Ibid.,* p. 248.

29. *Ibid.,* p. 294.

30. *Ibid.,* pp. 157-158, 160.

31. Rachilde, *loc. cit.,* LXV, 691.

32. *L'Ecole des mariages,* p. 241.

33. *Ibid.,* p. 10.

34. *Ibid.,* p. 39.

35. *Ibid.,* p. 125.

36. Rachilde, *loc. cit.,* p. 692.

37. "Les Romans de M. Edmond Jaloux," *Revue des Deux Mondes*, LVII (June 1, 1920), p. 699.

38. *L'Ecole des mariages*, p. 318.

NOTES TO CHAPTER IV

1. Edmond Jaloux, *Les Saisons littéraires: 1904-1914* (Paris: Librairie Plon, L.U.F., 1950), pp. 46-47.

2. Edmond Jaloux, *Le Démon de la vie* (Paris: J. Ferenczi, 1933), p. 52.

3. *Ibid.*, p. 28.

4. *Ibid.*, p. 51.

5. *Ibid.*, p. 53.

6. *Ibid.*, p. 117.

7. *Ibid.*, p. 163.

8. In discussing the interaction of Simone and Robert, Jules Bertaut made the following observation: "Jaloux a étudié avec patience les actions et les réactions de ces deux coeurs l'un sur l'autre." (*Le Roman nouveau* [Paris: La Renaissance du Livre, 1920]), p. 63. Bertaut's remark supports my feeling that human relationships now constitute a dynamic force which replaces the immobility of the early novels with a new sense of motion and of life.

9. *Le Démon de la vie*, pp. 156-157.

10. *Ibid.*, p. 100.

11. *Ibid.*, pp. 46-47.

12. Walter Lacher points out this resemblance when he states: "L'amour communion [de Déonat] fait penser à Gide, aux effusions des *Nourritures*." (*Le Réalisme dans le roman contemporain* [Geneva: Imprimerie Centrale, 1940]), p. 269.

13. *Le Démon de la vie*, p. 177.

14. Stated by Madame Edmond Jaloux during a personal interview with her, Lausanne, December 23, 1959.

15. Jens Peter Jacobsen (1847-1885): Danish novelist and poet who incorporated the Darwinian ideas of his time in the novel *Niels Lyhne* (1880), and who illustrated the problem of the atheist striving for his own moral unity.

16. Edmond Jaloux, *Les Saisons littéraires: 1896-1903* (Fribourg: Editions de la Librairie de l'Université, L.U.F., 1942), pp. 22-25.

17. The method that Jaloux uses in *Le Reste est silence* to resurrect the past through sense impressions is essentially the same as Proust's "rencontre". However, while Jaloux merely tried to recapture a bygone atmosphere, Proust analyzes these fleeting moments of encounter with his former self, and from that analysis derives a new philosophy of existence and of artistic creation.

In this connection, it is interesting to note Proust's warm feeling for this novel, as he wrote to Jaloux: "Je veux vous dire comme je viens de dévorer votre livre, comme je l'aime. Cette dernière nuit de l'enfant qui attend sa mère, le retour, le mensonge, et le regret de ne pas avoir serré la main de l'homme à la canne d'aigle, . . ." Edmond Jaloux, *Avec Marcel Proust,* suivi de dix-sept lettres inédites de Proust (Paris - Geneva: La Palatine, 1953), p. 120.

18. Maurice Betz, "Edmond Jaloux," *Biblothèque Universelle et Revue de Genève,* II (August, 1926), p. 190.

19. Armand Praviel, "Un Marseillais pessimiste: Edmond Jaloux," *Le Correspondant,* CCXCV N.S. 259 (April-June, 1924), p. 1006.

20. Edmond Jaloux, *Le Reste est silence* (Paris: Librairie Plon, 1921), pp. 124-125.

21. *Ibid.,* p. 54.

22. Edmond Jaloux considers the years of childhood as "une période où l'intuition étrange et la sensibilité sont des éléments essentiels." ("La découverte de l'enfant," *La Revue Universelle,* I [April-June, 1920]), p. 223-224.

23. *Le Reste est silence,* p. 140.

24. Emile Henriot, "Près de Lausanne: Edmond Jaloux est mort," *Le Monde,* (August 24, 1949).

25. *Le Reste est silence,* p. 80.

26. *Ibid.,* p. 129.

27. *Ibid.,* p. 29.

28. *Ibid.,* p. 15.

29. Henriot, *loc. cit.*

30. *Le Reste est silence,* p. 64.

31. *Ibid.,* p. 15.

32. *Ibid.,* pp. 120-121.

33. Yanette Delétang-Tardif, *Edmond Jaloux,* (Paris: La Table Ronde, 1947), pp. 80-81.

34. Edmond Jaloux, Introduction to *Deux ou trois grâces* by Aldous Huxley, (Paris: Librairie stock, 1931), p. xiii.

35. Daniel Mornet, *Introduction à l'étude des écrivains français d'aujourd'hui.* (Paris: Boivin et Co. 1939), p. 25.

36. *Le Reste est silence,* p. 154.

37. Francis de Miomandre brings out this dual aspect of the novel: "Avec *Le Reste est silence,* il y a une fusion plus intime des qualités de notre romancier. C'est le roman de moeurs familier, avec un accent personnel, et une profonde vérité humaine." (*Le Pavillon du Mandarin* [Paris: Emile Paul, 1921]), p. 260.

NOTES TO CHAPTER V

1. See *supra,* pp. 10-11.

2. *Cinquantenaire du Symbolisme,* préface par Edmond Jaloux (Paris:

Edition des Bibliothèque Nationales, 1936), pp. viii-x.

3. In a significant article on Bergson, Edmond Jaloux praised the philosopher's refutation of determinism as well as his emphasis on man's inherent freedom. In 1918 he wrote: "M. Bergson a rendu sa place à la liberté, que les déterministes nous avaient dérobée. Notre vie morale étant une suite d'états complexes qui se succèdent et s'interpénètrent, à tout moment le choix de l'individu intervient, à tout moment s'interpose un passé fait de mille volontés et de mille préférences." (*L'Esprit des Livres* première série [Paris: Librairie Plon, 1923]), p. 103.

4. J.-K. Huysmans, as early as 1884, had described this process in his famous novel *A Rebours,* through the sensuous experiments of its hero: Floressas des Esseintes. However this prototype of the decadent intellectual had sought the thrill of orchestrated and artificial sensations in reaction to the mediocrity of bourgeois life, while the later novelists of poetic imagination employed these sensations to rediscover a lost, but essential reality.

5. Edmond Jaloux, *Fumées dans la campagne* (Paris: La Renaissance du Livre, 1918), p. 5.

6. *Ibid.,* p. 1.

7. *Ibid.,* p. 2.

8. The nostalgic evocation of the past is an important theme of the symbolist movement. It recurs in the poetry of Verlaine and also in the verse of such late symbolists as Georges Rodenbach and Albert Samain. Guy Michaud discusses this obsession with the past in his chapter on "Les poètes du temps perdu" (*Message Poétique du Symbolisme* [Paris: Librairie Nizet, 1955]), III, pp. 492-501.

9. *Fumées dans la campagne,* pp. 188-189.

10. See *supra,* pp. 173-174, note 17 for a comparison between Proust's philosophical quest, and Jaloux's more modest attempt to revive the past.

11. *Fumées dans la campagne,* p. 272.

12. Ernest Raynaud brings out the lyrical quality of certain novelists who had come under the influence of symbolism and who tried to convey the complexity of human nature in *En Marge de la mêlée symboliste* (Paris: Mercure de France, 1936), pp. 199-220.

13. *Fumées dans la campagne,* pp. 99-100.

14. *Ibid.,* p. 29.

15. Paul Souday, "Fumées dans la campagne," *Le Temps,* (August 1, 1918).

16. *Fumées dans la campagne,* p. 270.

17. *Supra,* p. 47.

18. *Fumées dans la campagne,* p. 89.

19. *Ibid.,* p. 157.

20. *Ibid.,* pp. 151-152.

21. In his introduction to the Spanish translation of this novel, Blasco-Ibáñez exaggeratedly compares this personage with the figures of ancient

Greek tragedy; see his "Prólogo" (*Humos en el campo* [Valencia: Prometeo, n.d.]).

22. *Fumées dans la campagne*, p. 257.
23. *Ibid.*, p. 203.
24. *Ibid.*, pp. 177-178.
25. *Supra*, pp. 44-45.
26. *Fumées dans la campagne*, p. 48.
27. *Ibid.*, p. 282.
28. *Supra*, p. 25.
29. Gabriel Marcel noted the influence after 1914 of Henry James on Jaloux, particularly with regard to characterization and the shift of the "point of view" from the omniscient author to the perplexed narrator; personal interview with Gabriel Marcel, Paris, December 2, 1960.
30. James's *The Death of the Lion* was first printed in 1894.
31. Edmond Jaloux, *La Fin d'un beau jour* (Paris: La Renaissance du Livre, 1921), p. 115.
32. *Ibid.*, p. 76.
33. In a letter of Paul Claudel to Jaloux, the Catholic poet praised his colleague's symbolist descriptions of Versailles: "L'automne et vous procédez avec le même art par une fusion riche et savante de notes et de sentiments." Unpublished letter, Tokyo, December 6, 1921 (by kind permission of Mme Edmond Jaloux).
34. *La Fin d'un beau jour*, p. 172.
35. Albert Samain (1858-1900) the French poet and Georges Rodenbach (1855-1898) the Belgian symbolist are best known for their twilight scenes. Samain evoked the past splendor of Versailles; Rodenbach the fog-tinted scenery of his native Flanders.
36. Jules Bertaut brings out this anguish before the passage of time and the poet's innate gift of communicating that nostalgia in his chapter on "Jaloux" (*Le Roman nouveau* [Paris: La Renaissance du livre, 1920]) p. 71.
37. *La Fin d'un beau jour*, p. 201.
38. *Ibid.*, p. 203.
39. *Ibid.*, p. 265.
40. "Parmi les livres: La Fin d'un beau jour," *Revue de Paris*, (March 15, 1921), p. 383.

NOTES TO CHAPTER VI

1. A. Hernard, *L'Oeuvre de Freud et son importance pour le monde moderne*, Préface de Maurice Merleau-Ponty (Paris: Payot, 1960), p. 164.
2. Henri Mondor, a distinguished surgeon and literary critic, noted Jaloux's interest after the First World War in psychiatry in his "Portrait d'un humaniste," *Les Nouvelles Littéraires*, (January 14, 1954).

3. "(Observations sur la psychanalysee): Edmond Jaloux," *Le Disque vert*, numéro spécial (1924), p. 29.

4. Jaloux continued, beyond the 1920's, to feel the Freudian influence. *La Balance faussée*, a novel he wrote in 1931, analyzes the complexes and morbid jealousies of an unbalanced mind.

5. Wayne C. Booth takes important notice of the impact of the stream-of-consciousness technique on the evolution of the contemporary novel towards unstructured and amorphous plots. *The Rhetoric of Fiction* (Chicago: The University of Chicago Press, 1961), pp. 157-165.

6. Charles Du Bos stressed the importance of Jaloux's new psychological technique in changing the focus from an external to a purely subjective action in "Les Profondeurs de la mer," *La Nouvelle Revue Française* (February 1, 1923), pp. 448-449.

7. Edmond Jaloux, *Les Profondeurs de la mer* (Paris: Librairie Plon, 1922), p. 180.

7a. Georges Poulet explains this tendency of characters in modern fiction to create their personal, often incongruous sense of time (*Etudes sur le temps humain* [Paris: Librairie Plon, 1949]), pp. XLIII-XLVII.

8. *Les Profondeurs de la mer*, p. 151.

9. *Ibid.*, pp. 257-258.

10. *Ibid.*, pp. 257-258.

11. Joseph Place emphasizes the importance of Lothaire's spiritual quest in "Les Profondeurs de la mer," *Chronique des Lettres Françaises*, I (1923), p. 118.

12. "Mort de Virginia Woolf," in *D'Eschyle à Giraudoux* (Fribourg: Egloff, L.U.F., 1946), p. 256.

13. *Les Profondeurs de la mer*, p. 231.

14. *Ibid.*, p. 237.

15. *Ibid.*, p. 236.

16. Francis de Miomandre offers a searching analysis of Jaloux's half-tinted characterizations which must be touched up by the reader's own interpretation in "Les Profondeurs de la mer," *Les Nouvelles Littéraires*, (October 28, 1922).

17. *Les Profondeurs de la mer*, pp. 229-230.

18. James Ensor (1860-1949) the Belgian artist of Ostend was fascinated by masks. Jaloux greatly admired the painter's enigmatic world of the mask which illustrated human characteristics and which endowed the personages with universal truth.

19. François Fosca, "Edmond Jaloux et les littératures étrangères," *La Revue Hebdomadaire*, III (March-April, 1926), p. 493.

20. Ludwig Tieck (1773-1853): A German poet and writer of short stories whose *Märchen* express the hero's anguished solitude and his periodic trances or spells of madness. Jaloux discusses the atmosphere of terror which permeates the short stories of Tieck in his preface to *La Coupe d'or et autres contes de Ludwig Tieck* (Paris: Denoël et Steele, 1933), pp. x-xvii.

21. André Billy, "Soleils disparus," *l'Oeuvre*, (August 9, 1927); Franz Hellens, "Soleils disparus," *Rouge et Noir*, (October-November 1927).

22. Louis-Jean Finot, "Soleils disparus," *La Revue*, (September 1, 1927), p. 84; André Germain, "Soleils disparus," *La Revue Européenne*, (October 1927), pp. 380-382.

23. The theme of social vacuousness and of the hero's restless search for imaginary worlds recurs in Jaloux's other novels of the twenties, particularly in *Le Rayon dans le brouillard* (1924), and *O Toi que j'eusse aimée!* (1926).

24. Edmond Jaloux, *Soleils disparus* (Paris: Librairie Plon, 1927), p. 13.

25. Louis-Jean Finot emphasizes this coalescence of illusion and reality in "Soleils disparus," *loc. cit.*

26. *Soleils disparus*, p. 35.

27. "Francis de Miomandre, conteur féerique," in *D'Eschyle à Giraudoux*, p. 238.

28. *Soleils disparus*, p. 69.

29. *Ibid.*, p. 31.

30. *Ibid.*, p. 23.

31. *Ibid.*, p. 11.

32. *Ibid.*, p. 80.

33. *Ibid.*, pp. 81-82.

34. Christine Morrow shows that this nostalgia occurs in Jaloux's novels whenever he fuses elements of dream and of reality in her chapter on "Le Roman-rêve" (*Le Roman irréaliste dans les littératures contemporaines de langues française et anglaise* [Toulouse: Imprimerie Toulousaine, Lion Raoul, 1941]), p. 119.

35. *Soleils disparus*, p. 150.

36. *Ibid.*, p. 224.

NOTES TO CHAPTER VII

1. Jaloux expresses his belief in the relevance of Greek myths today in his chapter: "Actualité de la tragédie grecque" in *D'Eschyle à Giraudoux* (Fribourg: Egloff, L.U.F., 1946), pp. 11-19.

2. C. M. Bowra explains how the ancient Greeks used myths to clarify puzzling questions in his chapter on "Myth and Symbol" (*The Greek Experience* [London: Richard Clay and Co., Ltd., Weidenfeld and Nicolson, 1957]), pp. 103-122.

3. Northrop Frye brings this out in his discussion of myths and folktales in his article "The Archetypes of Literature" in *Myth and Literature: Contemporary Theory and Practice*, ed. John B. Vickery (Lincoln: University of Nebraska Press, 1966), 87-97.

4. Edmond Jaloux, *La Grenade mordue* (Paris: Librairie Plon, 1933), p. 174.

5. *Ibid.*, p. 179. In this instance Jaloux followed also the ritual connected with the Greek myth, for a close relationship existed between the notion of sacrificial offering and the myth of Persephone. See Martin P. Nilsson, *A History of Greek Religion* (Oxford: The Clarendon Press, 1925), pp. 88-91.

6. *La Grenade mordue*, p. 261.

7. *Ibid.*, p. 281.

8. *Ibid.*, p. 286.

9. *Ibid.*, p. 4. In this connection it is interesting to note Henri de Régnier's feeling that Séléré tried, above all, to perceive and communicate the hidden reality of people and of things; see his article ("La Grenade mordue," *Le Figaro*, [December 28, 1933]).

10. In his address before the *Académie française*, Jean-Louis Vaudoyer attributed this humanistic concept of art to Jaloux himself. Patrick Séléré undoubtedly reflects many aspects of the novelist's personality (*Discours de l'Académie française* [Paris: Firmin-Didot, 1950]), p. 25.

11. *La Grenade mordue*, p. 18.

12. Robert Graves emphasizes the more cheerful aspects of the myth of Persephone in *The Greek Myths* (Baltimore: Penguin Books, 1955), I 89-96, 120-125, II 107-110, 359. Jaloux however drew inspiration from the tragic overtones of the story.

13. Jean Debrix, "Les Livres: Quand Jaloux se critique lui-même," *Liberté*, (April, 1933); this imaginative identification of the myth with the individual case appears also in Jaloux's other novels of the 1930's: *Le Dernier jour de la création* and *La Chute d'Icare*.

14. *La Grenade mordue*, p. 216.

15. *Ibid.*, pp. 177-178.

16. *Ibid.*, p. 273.

17. See *supra*, pp. 117-121.

18. Norma Goodrich brings this out when she states: "In mythology there is . . . the feeling of a divine consciousness that orders the world in such a way that all happenings are purposeful, meaningful, and intentional." See her introduction to *Myths of the Hero* (New York: The Orion Press, 1962), p. xvi.

19. Werner Jaeger explains this concept of redemption through suffering in his discussion of the Oedipus legend in *Paideia: the Ideals of Greek Culture*, trans. Gilbert Highet (New York and London: Oxford University Press, 1945), I, p. 285.

20. A few years later, Sartre would conjure up such scenes to express the anguish of modern man in the face of chaotic and unaccountable existence.

21. In his autobiographical sketches, Jaloux describes the deep and abiding influence of Poe's short stories on his own search for unseen and imaginary worlds; see *Les Saisons littéraires 1896-1903* (Fribourg:

Editions de l'Université, L.U.F., 1942), pp. 14-15.

22. Edmond Jaloux, *l'Egarée* (Paris: Librairie Plon, 1938), pp. 14-15.

23. Christine Morrow emphasizes the growing influence of Poe on Jaloux, on the latter's quest for an invisible world; (*Le Roman irréaliste dans les littératures contemporaines de langues française et anglaise* [Toulouse: Imprimerie Toulousaine Lion Raoul, 1941]), p. 120.

24. Léon Daudet, "L'Egarée," *Candide* (March 17, 1938).

25. *L'Egarée*, pp. 92-93.

26. Robert de Traz brings out the subtle irony of Jaloux's portrayal and shows that Guelbert's dream of adventure disappears under the impact of erosive reality; see his article "Chroniques, Les Livres: L'Egarée," *Revue Hebdomadaire*, (March 26, 1938), p. 486.

27. Jaloux emphasizes the symbolic meaning of his character when he states that Alexandrine represents "a number of personages," in *L'Egarée*, p. 115.

28. *Ibid.*, p. 85.

29. *Ibid.*, p. 115.

30. *Ibid.*, p. 205.

31. Bowra, *op. cit.*, pp. 105-106.

32. It is interesting to note that Bergson, after reading *L'Egarée*, sensed the pervasive influence of fate in Jaloux's novel, and referred to this hidden force as ". . . une espèce de Fatalité à laquelle vos personnages s'abandonneraient." Unpublished letter from Henri Bergson to Edmond Jaloux, Paris, April 14, 1938 (by kind permission of Mme Edmond Jaloux).

NOTES TO CHAPTER VIII

1. Alfred Maubert, "Au bord du lac," *Les Nouvelles Littéraires*, (August 20, 1959).

2. In his article on Jaloux's later years, André Winkler analyzes the novelist's isolation from the younger generation of writers, see "Crónica de Suiza: Edmond Jaloux," *Insula*, Madrid, año IV, No. XLVII (November 15, 1949), p. 2.

3. René Etiemble, *Littérature Dégagée 1942-1953* (Paris: Librairie Gallimard, 1955), pp. 12-19 and *passim*.

4. Franz Hellens (1882-1972) pseud. of Frédéric van Ermengem: Brought up in a Flemish setting, but writing in French, this author reflects both the realism and mysticism of his native Belgium.
Henri Michaux (b. 1899-   ): Began to discover the world in 1920 as a seaman, established himself in Paris in 1924 where he alternated between the activities of writing and painting.
Louis Poirier — called Julien Gracq (b. 1910-   ): His fiction evokes the

terrifying atmosphere of Ann Radcliffe's Gothic novels as well as the magic world of dreams and of surrealism.

5. Oscar de Lubicz-Milosz (1877-1939): Born in Lithuania, Milosz went to Paris at the age of ten. Writing in French, he later expressed his mysticism in *Les Sept Solitudes* (1906) and in *Les Trois Symphonies* (1929).

6. Edmond Jaloux, *Le Culte secret* (Paris: La Table Ronde, 1947), pp. 12-13.

7. In a perceptive article, Robert Kemp shows that the death theme in this novel is inseparable from the characters' intimations of immortality, see "Edmond Jaloux le rêveur," *Les Nouvelles Littéraires*, No. 1069 (February 26, 1948).

8. Yanette Delétang-Tardif brings out the frequency of this conflict in the mystical personages of Jaloux's last period in her chapter "La clef du monde" (*Edmond Jaloux* [Paris: La Table Ronde, 1947]).

9. *Le Culte secret*, p. 142.

10. *Ibid.*, p. 145.

11. *Ibid.*, p. 101.

11a. See *supra*, chapter VII, pp. 120, 127, 128.

12. *Le Culte secret*, pp. 161-162. This secret which Catherine nurtures, and which slowly consumes her is due to her husband's morbid obsession of her death and to her own anguish in the presence of an unexplainable world.

13. Edmond Jaloux, *D'Eschyle à Giraudoux* (Fribourg, Egloff, L.U.F., 1946), p. 63.

14. *Supra*, pp. 115-118.

14a. It is interesting that the character's way of conquering the impermanence of the present closely resembles Mallarmé's mystical quest — the poet's search for eternity — which Georges Poulet brilliantly describes in his *Etudes sur le temps humain* (Paris: Librairie Plon, 1952), II, pp. 298-355.

15. *Le Culte secret*, p. 268.

16. *Ibid.*, pp. 60-61.

17. *Ibid.*, p. 129.

18. See *supra*, pp. 77-80, 89-91.

19. *Le Culte secret*, p. 62.

20. *Ibid.*, p. 132. It is interesting to note that Jaloux's somber vision of the castle of Draceynac resembles Gracq's eerie description of the *château d'Argol*.

21. Henrik Ibsen (1828-1906): Norwegian poet and dramatist whose most experimental play *When We Dead Awaken* (1899) marks a break with orthodox realism and a shift towards the symbolic drama of Strindberg.

22. Knut Hamsun (1859-1952) pseud. of Knut Pedersen: Norwegian writer who poetically expressed his closeness to nature and his love of

the earth in such works as *Under the Autumn Star* (1906), *A Wanderer Plays on Muted Strings* (1909), *The Last Joy* (1912), and in *Growth of the Soil* (1917).

23. Edmond Jaloux, *Le Pays des fantômes* (Lyons: Imprimerie Artistique en Couleurs, 1948), p. 53.

24. *Ibid.*, p. 156.

25. *Ibid.* pp. 21-22.

26. *Ibid.*, pp. 196-197.

27. Englebert, the hero of *La Grenade mordue*, awakens from his dream, and immediately senses the inflexibility of the concrete world. See *supra*, chapter VII, p. 117.

28. *La Pays des fantômes*, p. 27.

29. *Ibid.*, p. 61.

30. *Ibid.*, p. 195.

31. *Ibid.*, p. 57.

32. *Ibid.*, p. 60.

33. *Ibid.*, p. 76.

NOTES TO CONCLUSION

1. Francis de Miomandre, "Edmond Jaloux," in *Books Abroad,* University of Oklahoma Press, (January, 1950); Henri de Régnier, "La Grenade mordue," *Le Figaro,* (December 28, 1933); Benjamin Grémieux, "Edmond Jaloux," *La Nouvelle Revue Française,* dixième année (January-June, 1923), pp. 597-611.

NOTES TO BIBLIOGRAPHY

1. Articles arranged chronologically.

INDEX

183

Duhamel, Georges, 2, 167 n6

E

Ensor, James, 102, 177 n18
Erckmann-Chatrian, 36, 37, 170 n5
Erlande, Albert, 11, 12, 14
Estaunié, Edouard, 171 n5a
Etiemble, René, 180 n3
existentialism, 133

F

Fabre, Ferdinand, 16, 35, 36, 37,
  149, 170 n4
  Les Courbezon, 35
  Mon Oncle Célestin, 35
fatalism, 25, 122, 128, 129, 130,
  180 n32
fin de siècle, 14, 22, 50, 53
Flaubert, Gustave, 13, 19, 37, 40,
  70, 87
  Un coeur simple, 87
  Hérodias, 13
  Madame Bovary, 87
  Salammbô, 13
  La Tentation de saint Antoine, 13
Fort, Paul, 14, 19
France, Anatole, 21
Freud, Sigmund, 94, 95, 151, 176
  n1
Frye, Northrop, 178 n3

G

Gasquet, Joachim, 11
German Romanticism, 27, 151
Gide, André, 2, 11, 13, 14, 15-16,
  18, 24, 37, 54, 62, 95, 167 n4,
  168 n23, n24
  Les Cahiers d'André Walter, 11
  Les Faux Monnayeurs, 95
  L'Immoraliste, 15, 62
  Les Nourritures terrestres, 13, 15
  Paludes, 11
  Le Voyage d'Urien, 11
Gilbert de Voisins, Auguste, 11, 12,
  20, 55, 167, n6
Giraudoux, Jean, 76, 153, 165 IV,
  157 V
Gracq, Julien (Louis Poirier), 133
  Au château d'Argol, 133, 180,

181 n4

H

Hamsun, Knut (Knut Pedersen),
  11, 142, 181-182 n22
  Wanderers, 142, 181-182 n22
Hardy, Thomas, 11, 12
Heine, Heinrich, 27
Hellens, Franz (Frédéric van Er-
  mengem), 103, 133, 178 n21,
  180 n4
  Nouvelles Réalités fantastiques,
  133
Henriot, Emile, xii, 1, 2, 21, 24,
  167 n3, 171 n41
Hervieu, Paul, 21
Hinduism, 20, 89
Hoffmann, August Heinrich, vi, 8,
  27
  Contes fantastiques, vi, 8
Hofmannsthal, Hugo von, 28
Huxley, Aldous, 174 n34
Huysmans, J.K., 8, 9, 175 n4
  A Rebours, 9

I

Ibsen, Henrik, vi, 142, 181 n21
  When We Dead Awaken, 142
individualism - individual, 2, 28-29,
  55, 104, 153
interior monologue, 95, 99, 105,
  109, 116, 153
introspection, 57, 71, 81, 97, 105,
  122, 149, 150, 152
intuition, 65, 66, 68, 69, 70, 80,
  82, 83, 84, 85, 91, 100, 150
inwardness, 98, 99, 107, 109, 132,
  151, 153

J

Jacob, Max, 23-24
Jacobsen, Jens Peter, vi, 63, 173
  n15
  Niels Lyhne, vi, 63, 173 n15
Jaeger, Werner, 179 n19
Jaloux, Edmond
  birth,7
  childhood, 8, 36, 63
  death, 31, 171 n41

184

N

naturalism, 3, 8, 9, 42, 43, 48, 53, 54, 75, 76, 77, 87, 150, 171 n3
naturisme, 14
Nerval, Gérard de, 11, 103, 151
  Aurélia, 103
nihilism, 113, 144
Noailles, Anna de, 21
Nouvelles Littéraires (*Les*), 26
Novalis, vi, 27

O

occult (the), vii, 20, 136, 145, 146

P

pantheism, 27, 101, 137, 142
Paris, vii, 18, 19, 20, 24, 38, 55, 57, 86, 108, 116, 117, 125, 127, 135, 136, 169 n8
Péguy, Charles, 9
Peyre, Henri, 168 n20
Picasso, Pablo, 23
Poe, Edgar Allan, 8, 27, 123, 124, 126, 156 IV, 169-170 n13
  Contes extraordinaires, 8
  "The Fall of the House of Usher", 123
  "The Mystery of Marie Rogêt", 123
positivism, 22, 39, 40, 47, 49, 149
Poulet, Georges, 177 n7a, 181 n14a
Prix Fémina, 20
Proust, Marcel, 9, 24, 25, 66, 76, 153, 157 V, 156 VI, 168 n8, 170 n15, 173-174 n17
  Du côté de chez Swann, 66
  Les plaisirs et les jours, 170 n15
  A la recherche du temps perdu, 26, 80
provincial bourgeoisie, 37, 46, 50, 51, 67, 68, 149
psychoanalysis, 94, 95, 120, 151, 176 n2, 177 n3

R

Rachilde, 51, 170 n12, n24
Régnier, Henri de, vi, 9, 11, 14, 21, 24, 25, 148, 156, 179 n8
  Tel qu'en songe, 9
Renan, Ernest, 8
Richter, Jean Paul, vi, 27
Rilke, Rainer Maria, 27-28, 135, 136, 157 V, 161, 170 n31
  Duino Elegies, 136
  Sonnets to Orpheus, 136
Roberty, Henri, 12
Rodenbach, Georges, 14, 175 n8, 176 n35
Romains, Jules (Louis Farigoule), 95
  Lucienne, 95
romans de moeurs, 15, 16, 20, 35, 37-49, 50-54, 56, 67, 69, 79, 81-82, 93, 97, 153

S

Saint-Exupéry, Antoine de, 29
Saint-Georges de Bouhélier, 14
Saint-Pol-Roux, 19
Samain, Albert, 90, 175 n8, 176 n35
Sartre, Jean-Paul, 133, 179 n20
Schwob, Marcel, 168 n23
Shakespeare, William, 10, 12
Shelley, Percy Bysshe, 12
Sorel, Georges, 23
Souday, Paul, 82, 165, 175 n15
Soupault, Philippe, 95
  Les Champs Magnétiques, 95
space, 114, 139, 141
Stravinsky, Igor, 24
  Firebird Suite, 24
  Rite of Spring, 24
stream-of-consciousness, 28, 109, 151, 177 n5
Strindberg, August, vi, 181 n21
style, 37, 55, 67, 69, 71, 75, 77, 79, 85, 90, 92, 93, 95, 126, 150, 151, 176 n33
  characterization, 29, 39, 40-45, 47-49, 51-54, 57-63, 66-67, 69-71, 80-89, 91-93, 98-101,